Final Touchstones

Linda M. Romanowski

BROWN POSEY PRESS

an imprint of Sunbury Press, Inc.
Mechanicsburg, PA USA

an imprint of Sunbury Press, Inc.
Mechanicsburg, PA USA

For information about special discounts for bulk purchases, please contact Sunbury Press Orders Dept. at (855) 338-8359 or orders@sunburypress.com.

To request one of our authors for speaking engagements or book signings, please contact Sunbury Press Publicity Dept. at publicity@sunburypress.com.

FIRST BROWN POSEY PRESS EDITION: January 2023

Set in Adobe Garamond Pro | Interior design by Crystal Devine | Cover by Frankie Reed | Edited by Abigail Henson.

Publisher's Cataloging-in-Publication Data
Names: Romanowski, Linda M., author.
Title: Final touchstones / Linda M. Romanowski.
Description: First trade paperback edition. | Mechanicsburg, PA : Brown Posey Press, 2023.
Summary: *Final Touchstones* is an Italian heritage memoir in hybrid form. Each standalone piece tells one story of four brothers who leave Sicily for America in the early 1900s. The author's maternal grandfather is the seminal figure from age three to his emigration to a new life—a decision that changed his and his family's destiny forever.
Identifiers: ISBN : 978-1-62006-896-0 (softcover) | ISBN : 979-8-88819-024-1 (ePub).
Subjects: BIOGRAPHY & AUTOBIOGRAPHY / Cultural, Ethnic, and Regional | BIOGRAPHY & AUTOBIOGRAPHY / Personal Memoir | FAMILY & RELATIONSHIPS / General.

Product of the United States of America
0 1 1 2 3 5 8 13 21 34 55

Continue the Enlightenment!

To my beloved grandparents, my parents, and
my cousin Mary Bonanno.

Contents

———◦❀◦———

PROLOGUE

———⚬⊙⊙⚬———

This memoir attempts to portray my Italian American heritage in a hybrid prose/poem form of memoir. The primary thrust involves my relationship with my maternal grandparents, Gaetano and Sebastiana (Anna) Arcidiacono, who arrived in America from Sicily in the early 1900s. My paternal grandparents, Raffaele (Ralph) and Rosina (Rose) Marrone, play a lesser but significant role. These relationships expand to include family and friends addressed as "family," encompassing three generations, primarily from my perspective.

As we aged within our respective periods, my perceptions of these relatives, whom I still love deeply, changed. Do these perceptions become a factor in my relationship with them? How do I/we change toward one another within these perceptions? Do we change at all?

My reference to the I/we is an attempt to include the reader in my experience. I've asked myself many times why I wanted to write this memoir. Why does it matter? It matters because my generation, the Baby Boomers, is the last (with few exceptions) that has a direct, personal connection to those immigrants from the Great U. S. Immigration Wave of the early 20th Century. We knew these relatives, not just about them. Ours is the unbroken link to the fact, not to folklore.

Posts on social media gather ethnic groups of every persuasion. I follow *Facebook Italians, The Old School Italians, The Italian Families of the World,* and *I Love that I'm Italian.* These are magnets of family photos, food, and memory posts of customs that use the word "gravy" for sauce or vice versa. The focus widens as the Coronavirus revives scenes posted on *Vintage Philadelphia Photos*. It creates an unforeseen flood of commentary about those who succumbed during the Spanish Influenza epidemic. It has taken me forty years of writing family accounts to realize we carry a Heart Stone, an emotional touchstone. Social media points to a yearning for this connection.

I am part of a people who brought fig seeds, olive branches, and grapevine cuttings to America, taking the same chance they and their homeland treasures would survive here. We still have a thriving grapevine in Swedesboro, NJ, which we believe my maternal grandfather, great uncle, and friends planted. At the time of this writing, the oldest surviving member of my family was my mother's first-cousin, Mary Bonanno, who turned 100 years of age in May of 2021. She was my vital, living heart stone who passed away three months later.

The struggle of my family and others to remain in their new land without betraying their homeland or themselves is the struggle that brought the Greatest Generation into existence. Without this Greatest Generation, where would we be? Where would the world be?

My challenges lay within me a deeply personal, emotional, and intellectual journey. I wish to refrain from the melodramatic, the preachy, and the overly proud. How do I balance these non-fiction accounts, where the predominant weight rests upon my grandparents' lives? I want to present an arc of time, encompassing life events and lessons learned. Mine will not be an exceptional work per se, but it will be my own, filled with distinct elements, perceptions, and reactions. I do not want this work viewed as separating Italians/Sicilians as a group surpassing all others. My intention is not to elevate my heritage above any other legacy. Mine will be an attempt to present a way of life where the reader can seek common ground. An endeavor of substance, quiet beauty, humor, and a defined way of life through my lifetime experience, hardwired into memory. Not perfect, but real. Not exact, but as accurate as memory provides. A universal aspect of gratitude to relatives who unknowingly changed our lives. A meaningful testament to the bittersweet rather than to the remorseful.

I hope the focus is constant, the scaffold of heredity and my generation's connection to it. My life as a daughter and granddaughter appears in a generational approach. My parents are not as strong a presence in the memoir per se, but conduits that strengthened the bond between my grandparents and me. Without them, there would be no memoir.

I positioned my work in three sections: the Italian-Italian, the Italian-American, and the American-Italian, respectively. Each generation is in their own time, on paper, but not disconnected. I aim to relate each story as self-contained, written intentionally for each piece to stand independently. This structure provides an option for you, the reader, whether your preference is a straight-through experience or a selective one. In this way, repetition can ensure continuous flow without the need to thumb through previous pages for recollection. My attempt to add poetry is a motif, a weaving element throughout the prose.

My greatest hope is that you, the reader, might seek out an elderly family member to listen to his/her/your history and to glean wisdom from any oral recollections they might share. Note the light in their eyes, tone of voice, and laughter as they transform into yesteryear before your eyes. They are your vital, breathing resource, perhaps a Vesuvius of memory simmering in their far-back reaching world.

There is no cure for the ache of not knowing, of not asking while you can; sit quietly with your family matriarch/patriarch, preferably in a favorite place you share. Play music that means something to your loved one. While you can, before life parts you. Then, resolve what you learn to print or to any form of your choice.

I am grateful for your choosing my resolve to my ancestor's time in print.

Auguri! Cent Anni!

Linda M. Romanowski

Section I

❦

ITALIAN – ITALIAN

The Little Boy—1895

—◦⊙◦—

Only the nails remained to finish the job. The coffin, the long, small narrow box.

The sobbing woman did not know what she had done to deserve this. Her not knowing of this mystery illness. Her third son, who entered the world so strong and determined. His strapping cry as he announced his presence. Now, his moan was barely audible. His mother's wail, loud enough for both, this her preparation for prayer to implore Jesus to spare this young bambino.

The mystery of his illness is a mystery to everyone. He was only three years old; this hope that children bring, this hope of a way out of poverty. Nothing more could be done. The family was summoned. As they came, the last of the nails sealed the ends of the wood.

Acireale is a coastal city northeast of Catania, Sicily. It is situated at the foot of Mt Etna, meaning beautiful mountain, facing the Ionian Sea. This is the land of the Cyclops' Isles. In Greek mythology, Apollo slew the race of one-eyed giants because their thunderbolts killed his son. The place where the little boy's elderly aunt appeared was a place of strange stories and unexplained events.

The aunt glanced at the mysteriously sickly child, pale and listless. She looked at his long legs, at his face that could no longer summon tears. She had just spoken to the coffin maker, most likely a family member. The story relayed with tears. The aunt, a believer in old wives' tales, touched his pulse and listened for his heartbeat. She learned his fever came and went. She knew the doctor could do nothing more for him.

After pausing, contemplating, praying, and chanting, her thick brows drew together in a conference. Then she relaxed. She took a deep breath. She heard the clanging of the coffin maker's tools.

The moment of awareness struck her. *San Antonio!* she shrieked. She waved her arms, rolled up her sleeves, and asked for a bowl of water, a crust of bread, and a whole clove of garlic. She peeled the garlic in ritual, this sacred onion originated in Central Asia many centuries ago. Garlic, used for food preparation and medicinal purposes, is the drug of salvation for any epidemic that reared its head. She rubbed the cloves to remove the cellophane outer skin. She gently messaged the oil from each clove segment, rubbed the oil between her index finger and thumb on each hand. Lifting the lightly soaked bread, she chanted an Italian prayer. She rubbed her fingers and thumbs over the bread, kneading it. She held it sanctified between her palms.

The child's mother picked him up from the bed and brought him to the older woman. She anointed his forehead and his cheeks as if making the sign of the cross. Then, she touched the bread to his lips. His eyes fluttered open, and his lips parted, his facial features coming to alertness as he began to chew on the bread. He chewed hungrily as if recalling an ancient act, eyes pleading for more.

The elderly aunt looked at the astonished faces of her relatives, who had chanted the rosary throughout her ritual. She held the child in her arms, scolding them for their lack of faith, not in God, but in her. *Aglio! Aglio! Aglio!* (Garlic! Garlic! Garlic!)

The young boy made a miraculous recovery. The garlic had saved him. How could they not have known this? The family rejoiced. I'd venture a guess that the coffin became a garlic planter. Old wives' superstitions would never permit a death box to remain in its original state.

The three-year-old survived—Gaetano Arcidiacono, my maternal grandfather. I am here, bearing witness to an old wives' tale.

1900

Grandpop Arcidiacono (aka Arci, pronounced AR- CHEE) was eight years old at the turn of the twentieth century. He recalled those last few days of 1899, when people *talked pazzo*, crazy. One of his female relatives screamed incessantly. People cried that the world was coming to an end.

Italian ladies chanted Italian prayers over their children to ward off *il mal occhio*, the evil eye, if someone cursed them.

Grandpop knew when it was New Year's Eve. Acireale blazed with firesticks, shouts, singing, drinking, screaming, and dancing. No use trying to sleep.

He paused in his retelling and said, *I'm-a eighty-five-a years old. If somebody told-a me that day what I would do, what I would see in my life-a time, I would-a though-a he was pazzo!*

His youngest sister, Grazia (Grace), the eighth and last child born in the family, would be born in 1903. Their mother, Maria, brought children into the world in nineteenth and twentieth centuries. The world did not come to an end. A new world for Gaetano was about to begin.

Sons of Sicily

—⚬✿⚬—

Sebastiano Arcidiacono and Maria Grasso Arcidiacono brought eight children into the world, four girls: Josephina, Rosina (Rose), Agatha, and Grazia (Grace), and four boys: Rosario, Salvatore (Sam), Gaetano (my maternal grandfather), and Giovanni (John). They lived in Acireale, a coastal city northeast of Catania, Sicily. Their circumstances were modest, bordering on poor. Sebastiano was a stone mason who constructed ornate walls for the well-to-do. For all of its prestige, there was barely enough food to feed everyone. There were nights of hunger—interrupted sleep.

A tract of land was attached to the family's home, perhaps an acre or two, where herbs, vegetables, and flax were grown. Once harvested, the sisters spun the flax into thread. They hand-weaved the threads to linen, clothed the family, and made tablecloths and furniture scarves. An assumption of added income was possible. Sebastiano viewed his children more as laborers than progeny; education was not a priority. This frame of mind would alter the course of two of his sons forever.

⚬✿⚬

Rosario, the firstborn, was nine years Gaetano's senior. He was tall and stiff, a posture of arrogance and worldliness. He had his father's ear from as far back as Gaetano could remember. Their father conferred with him in all household matters, a fact not lost among his siblings.

One day, this eldest son and his father walked through the flax crop and caught sight of Gaetano. Rosario motioned to his father, *put Gaetano to work in this field. He is big and strong.* Their father immediately agreed. He nodded to his younger son to get to work *pronto.*

For an instant, life went out of Gaetano. He felt Rosario turn him upside down. He banished him from an education. He separated him from the rest of the family. He breathed in bitterness; he detested Rosario from that moment with uncharacteristic hatred. He thoroughly despised him as he would never hate or despise anyone else. Gaetano's venom was not toward his father but toward his brother's ability to exploit Sebastiano's calm nature. Rosario knew he could assume the patriarchal role without protest. His bravado continued well after the four brothers crossed the ocean. He attempted to inflict authority upon them when World War I broke out. Their brother Sam complied and fought in Turkey in the Gallipoli Peninsula Campaign (1915-1916). Gaetano, my grandfather, was married in 1915; my grandmother was pregnant with their first child. But that wasn't the real issue for his refusal to follow Uncle Sam. Gaetano vowed never to allow Rosario to interfere with his life again.

The oldest daughter, Josephina, aka Ida, shared Rosario's entitled nature. Ida played her own role in stunting the education of the youngest son, Giovanni (John). One day, when Uncle John came home from school, Ida ordered him to harvest the flax crop with grandpop. When he refused, she told their father, who, at her command, promptly removed him from the classroom. From that moment, John assisted their father in his stone masonry. His formal education terminated, stopped at the fifth grade. His hatred toward Ida twinned with grandpop's for Rosario. He refused to speak about Ida to anyone. When asked, his mouth would form a straight line across his face, his right index finger to his lips; he always shook his head *no.* Two brothers resolved to *Omerta*, silence. Uncle John learned to read by attending night school when he was well into adulthood, as much to spite Rosario as his desire to learn. Grandpop did not follow suit.

≈≫⊙≪≈

Grandpop Gaetano Arcidiacono, 1914   Grandpop Arcidiacono's parents,
                                        Maria and Sebastiano

Left to Right: Gaetano, Rosario, Salvatore (Sam), Giovanni (John) Arcidiacono,
1913

Body language in Italian culture is an overstatement. We talk with our hands; our hands are our souls.

Photographs are a silent language, a time-captured reinforcement. Expressive body movements are frozen. The photo of Grandpop Arcidiacono's parents shows a couple bound by duty, respect, and culture. My great-grandfather does not appear robust but sturdy and quiet-natured, a person who avoided confrontation. My great-grandmother shines with her silent wisdom and her husband's direct support. Her dress is matronly, traditional, and modest. Grandpop often impressed on me that he saw them as good people, bound to their homeland. They depended on their sons' securing their fortune in America to insulate them into their old age. Only one son, Rosario, returned permanently in 1920.

My Uncle John's arrival in America in 1913 marked his sixteenth birthday. The sons of Sicily photograph, taken that year, is the only known portrait of my grandfather with his brothers. This photo is one of attitude. Of Rosario, second from the left, his mustache dictates his opinion. A visible swagger resides in his eyes. His elevated foot, in a kick position, evokes power. I'm moved to kick him mentally every time I look at him. The beautiful ancient Roman-style chair held his regal posture. Uncle Sam was seated beside him, his masculine gloves in his elegant right hand. His kind face, he was always so kind to us. Grandpop is standing beside Rosario, their obvious tension in black and white. No physical contact exists between them. Three of them in various stages of their prime. Uncle John, a teenager, hand on Uncle Sam's shoulder. Uncle Sam holds no tobacco. This is the first and last iconic picture of that generation of male Arcidiacono lineage.

Field Exile

The oldest son caressed
their father's ear
and said to harness
grandpop to the land

Gaetano, banished to the field,
to learn to read Italian
on his own
to barely learn to write.

The heat of the earth
burned through
from feet to heart
He cut flax
as if to cut
his sibling's throat

He cursed him
every moment
in his sweat
his venom woven
into the clothes he wore
he swore
to never heed his word again.

(Perhaps the seed to stay
across the sea
germinated then)

The Italian Dream—1910

—◦⟨∞⟩◦—

When did they decide who was going to America, and why was that person chosen? There were eight children in the family, four girls and four boys. Where were they looking to go; where were they planning to stay?

When did they decide that their adopted village of South Philadelphia would not be the ultimate destination for the four brothers who left Sicily from 1907 to 1913? They planned to make their fortune and return home. Perhaps the family felt sending sons to America in their early prime would bring higher wages and a quicker return.

The twist in the ocean surfaced when the oldest son, Rosario, decided to return. This land of the adopted village was not for him. I know not why Salvatore (Sam) changed his mind not to join him. The third son, Gaetano, my grandfather, told the story that set his course to his permanently adopted village. The voyage to America was difficult. Stormy, choppy waters. Swelling, nauseating, rising tides were foreign to him. His physical strength and build were no match to the ceaseless pounding and swirling waves. He would use the word *steerage*, which I, his fifth grandchild, wholly misinterpreted. The insightful moment came when I realized he wasn't "steering" the ship. He was not a crew member; he was a cramped passenger, like cattle, in steerage—the part of the boat, the lowest level, meager provisions at a meager cost. The shock of the image of what he was not a rude awakening. They probably saw little of the light of day. Perhaps darkness was welcome.

Rumors floated throughout the ship about the Turkish army, causing unrest. Turkey's Ottoman government was weak. The thought of conscription into their army had he ventured back to Sicily was real. Gaetano was a tall, well-built, able-bodied eighteen-year-old, a quick pick for an invading Turkish troop.

Soon after arriving in America, Gaetano noticed the young woman taking care of her brother, a coworker. It was love at first sight, without question. The lovely Sebastiana sunk his heart. He visited her brother on pretense of seeing her. By then, this young man was set in his adopted village forever. Mount Etna, a beautiful mountain not far from his home, would fade in his memory and re-flourish whenever he spoke of an eruption he witnessed as a child.

How did the family react upon learning they would never see Gaetano again? Had I been there, would I have persuaded him to stay in Sicily from the start? Would I have exacted a promise, if he went back, that he would return to his adopted village?

Gaetano remained in America. The voyage, the Turks, and Sebastiana, the beautiful young woman, shifted the tide of his thinking. He never returned to Acireale. Would there be any doubt that I would be here?

The Point of No Return

On an April morning,
quite possibly the third,
you readied for the voyage
you swore of your return

To go to that majestic place
streets paved with gold
so you were told
your fortune in the making

For it was 1910, you, not yet twenty
no plan to stay across the sea for long
not much to take with you
except your name

full of letters a president will mispronounce
one day   that moment a century away
no matter now—the ship was waiting

I never asked about that day
only the day you arrived
April 22, 1910, 10:30 am, you said
you landed in Boston

then to New Jersey
then to South Philadelphia
then with Grandmom
our family began.

I never asked who held your
hand in Sicily   that   last
time   unknown to all
the last time

Was your mother too distraught
to stand along the shoreline
your four sisters   your brother   your father
left behind   were they there?

Did she know in her heart
this was the last time she would see her son?
(all little Italian ladies know what's
in their heart is true and quiet)

Voyage

<hr/>

When grandpop left Sicily on or about April 3, 1910, he had every intention of returning to his hometown of Acireale, a coastal city of Catania, southern Sicily. The town rests at the foot of Mt. Etna, facing the Ionian Sea. His brothers, Rosario, and Salvatore (Sam), were already in Philadelphia, PA. They fully intended to secure their fortune in America, then return to the family. He made the trip with a family friend at seventeen and a half years of age. He traveled on the "Lazio," a trans-Atlantic passenger ship. The ship traveled twelve to thirteen miles per hour, a speed he had never experienced. The trip cost thirty-five dollars. The passport was twenty dollars. Grandpop estimated there were 500 to 700 Italians on the boat. He told me the US government gave the Italian government one dollar for every Italian who *crossed over*, as grandpop said. He traveled steerage class in the ship's lower deck, where the cargo is stored.

Grandpop arrived in Boston, Massachusetts, on April 22, 1910, at 10:30 am. He did not embellish his arrival. The voyage was very rough, terrifying to a young man who had never set sail. The steerage passing intensified seasickness; passengers viewed as breathing cargo, conditions so wretched grandpop never described it. When his unsteady feet touched the ground, he had never been so grateful.

One day, to change the subject but return to the topic, he described a different scenario, Ellis Island, one port that could have been any port.

Grandpop termed Ellis Island and all incoming immigration ports the "Gate of Tears." Any person who did not pass the entering physical registration must return to their mother country immediately. He heard stories but never knew if those ejected passengers would return to their original exit point. There were no age exceptions. Parents returned to Italy with sick children; unaccompanied children went back alone. Grandpop never shared that he saw any such deportations, but the possibility that his fate awaited this inspection was ever-present before him. It was far more terrifying than the crossing over to America.

The most feared diagnosis was trachoma, a highly contagious eye infection spread by handshakes, saliva, and contaminated surfaces. It could cause blindness and lead to death. When he shuddered while describing this, one could only imagine the horror. He would say no more about it. He and his three brothers passed their medical trials, arriving in the U.S. in different years and in different places.

Arrival

The first food Grandpop consumed in America was bananas. Five dozen for a nickel. He and his travel companion, a family friend, stuffed themselves with their unexpected bounty until their stomachs, bloated with fresh fruit goodness, could hold no more.

He roared with laughter as he relayed this story. He wiped tears from his eyes. For a week, he couldn't "move his panza," his belly. No *cacca*, fecal matter.

He boarded at a place where he cooked for himself; the proprietor did his laundry, with one or two shirts ironed each week. Eventually, he and his friend traveled to Swedesboro, New Jersey, to another friend's farm to pick asparagus. A relative and a friend planted a grapevine smuggled from Italy. The grapevine still survives, its bounty ever sweet.

Sebastiana's Family

———⊷⟁⟁⊷———

Grandmom Arcidiacono's stoicism left much to mystery and conjecture. Her death certificate indicates she was born in Italy, but my recent discovery of her birth certificate lists her birthplace as Mascali, Sicily. It is located in the metropolitan city of Catania, approximately eleven miles northeast of Acireale, grandpop's hometown. She arrived in America in 1912, or thereabouts, as they met through her brother, Antonio (Tony). A sister, Caterina (Catherine), accompanied her. They left behind their parents, a brother (Leonardo), and a sister (Maria).

Grandmom never mentioned Maria's name; she never spoke of her family. My only memory of Uncle Tony is of his death. After their marriage, my grandparents separated from him, as he was a harsh man. His death caused my grandmother great sorrow. Bad temperament or not, he was her brother, her only masculine family link in her New Land.

Her greatest familial comfort was Aunt Catherine, her sustaining link to their past life. Their quintessential greeting, *amoti Sorella,* beloved sister, persisted through their lifetimes. It always moved me to see this ritual gesture. I loved Aunt Catherine, above all other reasons, for her devotion to grandmom.

Grandmom never mentioned her voyage to this country. I've always imagined her, seventeen-year-old Sebastiana Messina, terrified. Her quiet, reserved nature suggested this. Most likely, she clung to Aunt Catherine during the trip, particularly during periods of rough travel. Only now do I consider the origin of her thunderstorm phobia linked to this voyage. Mom often remarked on grandmom's overbearing protection of her children when dark clouds gathered. I saw her hide in the coat closet on one occasion.

I never asked her about her family. Somehow, I sensed she would not have responded. Somehow, early on, I knew my questions would cause her great sadness. The only comment she shared was that we were descendants of a king of Sicily.

In the photo, I ascertain the young lady standing to our left is Aunt Caterina, Aunt Maria in the middle, and Sebastiana (grandmom) on the right. Their parents are seated in front of them, made smaller by their pose. There is no family picture of or with her brothers that I have ever seen. The photo below might be the only one of the five of them together, between 1910 and 1912, perhaps a farewell composition before the two daughters left the country. Aunt Catherine might have returned for a visit, but grandmom never did.

From Left, Back Row: Caterina (Catherine), Maria, Sebastiana (Grandmom). Foreground: Grandmom's parents, Orazio and Josephine Messina.

From Field to Mill

⁂

Many weaving jobs were temporary or seasonal, but the mill permanently employed the three brothers. They rose to the level of the top three weavers in the company. Rosario did not join them; his employment remains unknown. He returned to Italy in 1920.

Uncle John, the youngest, remained at the mill until his retirement in the mid-1960s. When the unions began visiting the textile industry, he welcomed them. Uncle John misunderstood his unmatched skill as an entitlement to speak his mind in operational matters. He voiced his support for the unions and his reward was the third shift in the weaving schedule, the twilight shift, from 3:30 pm to midnight. His brothers retired, and he faced his remaining employment years without them, without the camaraderie of the day shift workers. Cousin Mary reasoned that this dramatic work shift ruined her parent's relationship. They separated after forty-eight years of marriage. My cousin reached this conclusion for the first time during our conversation on September 21, 2020. Now I wonder if his brothers had been there when the unions arrived if they would have done all they could to prevent him from asserting his misperceived authority.

An Ill-Timed Move

⸻⟡⸻

My maternal grandfather, Gaetano Arcidiacono, was a young man in a new land when he arrived in America on April 22, 1910. He came through Boston in that city's second wave of The Great Immigration (1880-1921). He planned to earn his fortune in this country with his three brothers and return to Sicily. There were several reasons why this plan did not materialize. His primary change of heart, which fate ordained, resulted from meeting a beautiful young woman, Sebastiana (Anna) Messina, when he was twenty.

Their courtship began slowly, in a haphazard fashion. Anna's sole purpose for being in America was to take care of her brother, my Uncle Antonio (Tony). Tony and Gaetano had formed a friendship through a mutual acquaintance at the mill. Gaetano had no idea that Tony had a sister until he stopped by his boarding house one weekend. Once Gaetano saw Anna, life as he knew it would change once again, forever.

He was immediately smitten with this petite, quiet young lady whose braided chestnut hair taunted his dreams. He needed a ruse to see her. He visited Tony on the premise of borrowing one of his books. Anna knew the real reason Gaetano came was to see her because she realized early on that he could barely read. Time passed, and their schedules collided more than they coincided, yet they discovered their true home would be in one another someday.

As more time passed, Gaetano noticed Anna grow weary. Taking care of Tony and working at a nearby factory proved more than she anticipated. Homesickness for the rest of their family in Sicily made her days overwhelming. The outside world was loud and intimidating. The radio was the comforting link to her Old World, opera music and Italian speech, the loving sounds that kept despair at length. This, and her Italian cooking, gave her solace. The sounds and the smells of the familiar became a comfort in an unfamiliar place. When her brother came home from work as he always did—tired, dirty, and testy from working in the fabric mill, Anna gave him her full attention and devotion. She would not allow him to see her so distraught.

Gaetano considered ways to ease Anna's drudgery. His means were limited; he persevered until an idea came to mind.

He had not yet told her that he loved her. A man of few words, he thought a gift from him would provide a language of its own. One that would assure that his intentions toward her were genuine. He sought something which denoted pride, grace, and beauty. Something that conveyed that she was special. Something that Anna would know would come from his heart.

The idea came to him. He waited for a beautiful spring Sunday afternoon. Gaetano knew Tony would be home that day, so much the better for him and Anna since courtship visits in Sicily were conducted in the presence of family.

When Anna greeted Gaetano, she immediately noticed the peak season floral bouquet, a diminutive, cheerful array covering a box. He had presented her with flowers on initial social calls, but this was the first time there was something more than flowers accompanying them.

Anna set the flowers on a nearby table. Slightly flustered, she opened the box, took one look, and knocked the lid to the floor. Anna could feel herself flush, her face a hive of red patches. She dropped the box to her feet, pointing in disgust. Gaetano was speechless.

A pair of women's dress shoes brightened the room. Leather. Costly. Beautifully designed and constructed. A closed shoe with a modest heel. In Gaetano's favorite color, red. Anna was aghast, face as blush red as his gift. She continued pointing, blurting out Italian syllables. One word

Gaetano heard was *puttana*. Puttana, a woman of the night. A prostitute. Anna waved her blotched red arms at him to keep him at a distance. Gaetano, too flabbergasted to move, saw her tears of anger.

After Anna slammed her bedroom door, Tony enlightened Gaetano and explained her reaction. Bewildered and embarrassed, Gaetano learned that giving a woman a pair of shoes before marriage was a sign that the giver and the receiver were involved in premarital acts ascribed to a woman of ill repute. The shoe color he chose was an undeniable bellwether. I can only imagine my grandfather leaping from the chair to uphold my grandmother's honor. Tony knew their relationship was sacrosanct. Perhaps he wondered why Gaetano hadn't discussed this with him first.

Two generations later, I know why. Grandpop was a quiet, private, humble man. He kept his passions close to his vest. He was six months shy of his eighteenth birthday when he left his homeland. There was no time for him to learn about social graces. His was a life of manual labor, the mores of courtship a distant horizon. When he left Sicily, he left his sisters behind; Agatha was his confidant. Had Agatha been with him, she would have guided this shy, handsome brother so reluctant around women. Had Agatha been with him, she would have set him straight. There was no woman his age in his new surroundings that he would trust to tell him any better. Had he been treated with respect by the shoe seller, he would have retimed his purchase. Perhaps the seller believed he was married; not all men wore wedding bands, especially laborers.

My grandmother probably eavesdropped during Tony's lecture to her beloved. Her anger did not blind her to grandpop's sweetness, to his romantic nature toward her. His no-good-deed-going-unpunished was a lesson to her. She pulled herself and her pride together and opened her bedroom door. She picked up her gift, gathered the flowers, and patted grandpop's arm with her free hand.

The Proposal

———— ❧ ————

One day, someone somehow found Grandmom Arci in a receptive mood and asked her how Grandpop Arci proposed to her. Logic places the event a few months before their September wedding. In those days, engagements were not lengthy. Early spring sets the rainy atmosphere, the perfect ruse for another milestone moment in Gaetano's life. He prepared for every possibility for escorting Anna safely home.

While Gaetano was the consummate gentleman, he was no fool. He took full advantage of the precipitation. He sensed Anna beside him, never so close as she was at this moment. They walked so effortlessly together. Crossing the damp-smelling streets was a surprisingly pleasant experience for him as he directed her over the curbs and around neglected bottles. He kept her by his side, close enough to be polite, close enough to be protective, close enough to feel their steps in tandem.

Gaetano, always a methodical thinker, realized the opportune moment before him. He smiled in secret, thanking the rain for this encounter. Opportunity reigned; he took a deep breath. He needed to tip the umbrella forward to look down at Anna. He was at least a foot taller than she. The weather permitted Gaetano to pull Anna closer to him. He could be bold without appearing so.

He did not release his grasp when he said to her, *Anna, I want you to marry me.* Anna took a step back, looked up at him, and said, *Who, me?*

Our family reaction to this exchange followed a pattern of speech-lessness and laughter. Grandmom endured much teasing from us. Our *Who, me?* imitations of her response made her laugh. During their fiftieth wedding anniversary party, she blushed as if she returned to the *Who, me?* moment again.

I saw grandmom's gratitude for the rain in photographs of their later years. How often she looked up to grandpop with a smile. He gazed down at her, his face beaming his devotion. The same photo pose, he on the left, she on the right, unswerving body language. The only difference to be found is in their clothing and the background scenery.

Sometimes, I would see grandpop smile to himself when it rained. Surely he was grateful for more than the moisture nourishing his Victory Garden.

September 4, 1915

———◦◦◦———

On September 4, 1915, my maternal grandmother, Sebastiana Messina, married Gaetano Arcidiacono. As we sat outside our home one summer night, grandpop told me about that day. The evening heat must have reminded him—he told me it was sweltering. My poor grandmother, pretty, petite, and plump, wore a heavy white long-sleeved gown, her veil to the floor. In those days, bridal flowers were not handheld bouquets; they were horse blankets of white blossoms. It was a wonder anyone could have seen her face, surrounded by an apishamore of foliage and fabric. No one took any wedding photographs as far as the family knew. My Cousin Mary had no recollection of seeing any pictures. There was never an appearance of a single print or a wedding album.

I know they stood as a vision of love and beauty that day. I did not know that he did not dance with grandmom during the celebration until he told me. His lack of ability, in my Leenda mind, was a stunning revelation. My mind switched back to the adult one; in truth, I never did see him dance. For all the music, singing, and dancing surrounding our daily life, no memory of a two-step of his existed. When I asked him what they did during the party, he smiled and told me he drank beer, sang, laughed, and smoked with the male guests. He saw me frown. *Leenda, I loved beer, but soon after the wedding, I couldn't drink it anymore.* This intolerance seemed to hit him overnight. Wine and whiskey shots became his lifetime mainstays. He did not comment much on not dancing with his new *sposa,* spouse.

Then I thought back to when I asked grandmom about their wedding day. She told me they didn't dance, but not that he *couldn't.* Grandmom entertained herself by looking out the window and watching her guests outside. She did not wish to dance with any female guests. I knew better than to ask about her dancing with a man. The mere thought of my asking her that question would have horrified her. Italian married ladies never danced with anyone but their spouses. Except for male relatives, to a limited extent.

Grandpop remains the only Italian man I ever met who could not dance. His descendants inherited his *sposa's* dancing gene and her artistic talents, singing included. Their son, my Uncle Franzi, was a very talented drummer. Allegedly, when he was a young man, he played a set with Gene Krupa, his idol.

When their son, Sebastiano (Ben), was born nine months later, the proof that grandmom did not gaze through the window all night revealed itself.

Shadow Dancing

Grandmom glanced out the window
watched her wedding guests dancing
sighed   no doubt   glad
she married a good man
good in all things
except dancing.
Shadows on the wall
invited her to join
and so   she did
movements twin to her own.

Someday she will have twins
of her own
when she and grandpop
stepped   as one.

The Decision

No one can say where old wives' tales originated. For those who have scoffed at many of those tales, many have repented. Those doubters realized a particular element of truth and knowledge in these beliefs. Formal education does not guarantee that those methods of study are the only ones that bear witness.

The young woman sat down among her friends, bracing her back against the wall. They gave her space to situate herself; they noticed those tell-tale signs of swollen ankles and slightly watery eyes. One of them gave her a damp cloth to wipe her brow. The women looked at her and waited for her to speak. She sighed *Sono incinta*. (I'm pregnant). One of the older women patted her shoulder, asking to place her hand on her abdomen. *I know already,* the young woman nodded, *Twins.* The news brought exclamations and clasped hands, some of those hands clasped in prayer. None of these women asked how she knew this. *They* knew; *she* knew. These were young Italian ladies, immersed all their lives with those unfailing perceptions based on lessons and observations learned from their little old Italian lady relatives. The young woman's diagnosis went unquestioned. They did not know the struggle of her question: should she end this pregnancy?

On that very day, the young woman's husband visited the neighborhood pharmacist. He was a pleasant man, Italian, as were his customers; he knew them all by name. Their children's names too. It was never an imposition on his time to greet them and sneak treats to those little ones who visited with their parents.

On that day, when he saw the young woman's husband, he immediately knew his visit would not be simple. The young man fidgeted, looked over his shoulder, and looked down at the floor. The pharmacist stepped out from behind the counter and motioned him to sit with him on one of the two chairs nearby. The young man held his head in his hands, unable to look at him directly. He slowly shook his head and told the pharmacist about his pregnant wife. The pharmacist, knowing the family, knowing they were parents of two children, knowing one child had died seven years ago, put his hand on his shoulder. The young man told him of their struggles; it was 1927. Though they were holding their own, they were unsure about this pregnancy. When the pharmacist heard there were twins, he did not doubt it. He asked about his wife, and those few questions poised him to brace himself. The young man said *We need to end this. How do you say it?*

The pharmacist took the deepest breath imaginable. He paused, calmed himself, looked the young man in the eyes, and said, *Do not consider this! She is showing. It is too late. I will not assist you if you ask me to give you something to end it. The Bambini are too far along; anything you might do now will probably kill her too. Twins—too dangerous!*

The young man expected as much. He held back his tears. He knew the pharmacist was right. He felt paralyzed. The pharmacist said *I know how hard this is. But think of your wife's health, think of your sons, think of those Bambini. You will survive this; good times and bad times come at the same time. These children will be your blessing.*

The young man thanked him. He pondered his words on the way home. He never considered that he might lose his spouse if they went through with an abortion. He tenderly spoke to his spouse about the visit. Their tear-filled eyes were comforted by their tightly held hands. His spouse stood up, placed her hand on her husband's face, and said, *We will bring these children into the world!*

On September 30, 1927, the twins were born. Maria and Vincenzo. *This one is mine. Papa's Doll-ee!* the delighted young man exclaimed as he cradled the black-haired perfect infant girl in his arms.

So, the twins arrived, and so did I, in the next era. Maria was my mother.

Of Washington and Lincoln

---◦◦◦◦---

The interrogator tried to trip Grandpop Arci up, no doubt worn out by all the waiting faces. He leaned forward and asked: *Who was the first president of the United States?* He leaned back and waited for Grandpop's answer. The heat in the room was unbearable.

George Washington, Grandpop replied. A thin line of sweat trailed down the back of his neck. His clean white shirt damped with each passing second.

The man leaned forward. He couldn't have been much older than this nervous immigrant, who probably was in his late twenties. *No, it isn't. It was Abraham Lincoln.*

Grandpop knew he was mistaken. He went over the citizenship questions many times with a family friend. He remembered Washington's face on a one-dollar bill, one seldom located in his pocket. He paused and looked at the man whose sneer was unmistakable. The questioner asked grandpop again. Again, he refuted grandpop's unwavering response.

Grandpop realized this man stood between him and his American Dream. Returning to Sicily was no longer an option. Always the soul of calm, despite frustrating perspiration, he said again, when asked, *Its-a George-a Washington.*

At this point, he broke out of his reverie to tell me how he knew his response was correct. Grandpop recalled how his family talked about Abraham Lincoln as the first assassinated US president. His voice slightly shook when he said he was born in 1892; he knew about the Civil War. His lack of education did not deter him from reasoning the relatively short time span between 1865 and 1892. He returned to his recounting.

You, you, are you calling me a liar? The clerk rolled up his sleeves; eyes narrowed, face reddened.

At that moment, Grandpop stood up. The tall, powerfully built, patient young man could stand it no longer. The noise, the crowds, the unforgiving heat, and the sniping mouth of the native-born American were more than he could bear. The interrogator felt grandpop's move—an electric current of power, their eyes at eye-level for a moment when he leaned forward. The interrogator misinterpreted grandpop's desire for relief as a move to strike him. He reared back on his chair full tilt and bellowed, *Ok, so it was George Washington!*

Grandpop looked at me, recovering from this past life exchange. He let out a sigh. *He tried to fool me, but Leenda, I knew, I **knew** the right-a answer!* There seemed to be a tear in his eye as he spoke.

Stress of Allegiance

———◦⊙◦———

My cousin Mary recalled that all Italians in America were asked by their relatives in Italy and Sicily to donate their jewelry, gold rings specifically, to Mussolini. It was during the mid-1930s. The dictator needed to increase his war chest; these rings were the perfect solution to fulfill this objective. Italians, passionate about their eighteen-carat accessories but wanting to do their part, willingly complied.

While searching through my family strongbox, I found a letter/receipt from the Italian Consulate General located in Philadelphia, PA, addressed to grandpop Arcidiacono, dated February 10, 1936. This correspondence, via my use of Google Translate, reads:

Dear Sir:

In applauding your patriotism, please note receipt of the objects that you generously donated to the homeland to which he describes as indicated below.

In assuring you that the aforementioned items will be transmitted to the Royal Embassy, I rename you, my Lord, the acts of my distinguished consideration.

The Consulate General
(Items listed)
Two gold bracelets
One gold ring

One gold chain with pendant
One gold chain
Two gold pendants
One broken gold ring
One gold cross
One woman's gold pin
One gold tie pin

～◦○◦～

I do not know if any of these items was my mother's jewelry. She was nine years old in 1936. Some pieces could have been gifts to celebrate wedding anniversaries; my grandparents had been married for 21 years. In this list of memories, there are eleven symbols of their lives together.

Cousin Mary's parents followed suit. Uncle John, her father, sent Mussolini her initial ring, given to her by him and her mother when she was eight. She recalled that her maternal grandmother donated her gold wedding band. She felt it patriotic to give to *the other side.* She told my cousin, *you don't-a forget-a your roots.* Cousin Mary still remembers her gold oval-shaped birthday gift, her elegant initials, *M A*, initialed on its surface.

There was a less formal way to collect these beloved jewelry pieces. Cousin Mary witnessed jewelry collectors gathering donations from groups of Italians at outdoor venues. Her memory is unclear if they visited the Italian neighborhoods or the Italian market. A brass one replaced every donated gold ring. A ring without shine, a shrewd acknowledgment of sacrifice. This collective operation did not function without attention to the culture, dispensed with the knowledge that no Italian married woman would continue living with a bare third finger on the left hand. Not for her or her husband.

Imagine the angst during this time, with the Second World War on the horizon. Imagine the innate goodness of Italian families on this side of the ocean, rationalizing that their offerings went beyond assisting Il Duce; it reached *their loved ones*, disconnected, on the *other side* of that same ocean. Imagine the escalation of emotion during World War II; the allies attacked every region of Italy, Sicily the ideal landing zone for invasion, the southern area in particular. Sons and brothers in America against sons and brothers in Italy, a Mt. Etna of emotion. Then, the country switched to the Allies in 1943. Their homeland alliance shifted to America. Did it bring relief? Did it bring regret in assisting a scoundrel? The subject is closed now, secure in my grandparents' minds and souls, forever in their graves.

⋘◦⊙◦⋙

I recently realized one treasure my grandmother held back, a precious, lovely pair of pierced earrings. Each earring appears as a dainty flower, with a tiny light blue stone positioned in the center prong. These earrings were for her first daughter, Maria, born in February 1920, who lived for only seven days. She died of pneumonia. Tradition ruled that a baby girl's ears were pierced at birth or close to the Baptism. Her condition and newborn death cast the ceremony aside. Maria was never baptized.

One day, my grandmother went to the server, which stood between her dining and living rooms. She placed an object in my hands, a small card that held Maria's earrings. Maria never wore them, an old-fashioned pair of screw-back adornments with a tinge of rose gold on their surface. I wore them as my "something old" on my wedding day. I wore them on my college graduation day and other special occasions. I will wear them, God willing, for my master's ceremony and the Rosemont College Centennial celebration. Touchstones a century in the making.

I still think of Cousin Mary's nostalgic moment of a phone conversation about her sacrifice, made without her knowledge. *She said it was the right thing to do at the time, but it still hurts.*

CONSOLATO GENERALE DI S. M. IL RE D'ITALIA
PHILADELPHIA, PA.

10 Febbraio 1936-XIV

126 S

- -1 RR

Ill.mo Signore,

　　　　　Nell'applaudire al di Lei patriottismo,
pregiomi segnare ricevuta degli oggetti che Lei generosa-
mente dona alla Patria e che ni descrive come indicato
qui in calce.

　　　　　Nell'assicurarLa che i predetti oggetti
verranno trasmessi alla R. Ambasciata, Le rinnovo,
Ill.mo Signore, gli atti della mia distinta considerazione.

Il R. Console Generale

due braccieli di oro
un anello di oro
un laccetto di oro con ciondolo
un laccetto di oro
due ciondoli di oro
un anello di oro rotto
una crocetta di oro
uno spillo di oro da donna
uno spillo di oro per cravatta

Ill.mo Signor
　　Gaetano Arcidiacono
　　632 Vernon st.
　　Philadelphia Pa;

Donation receipt

Baby Maria's earrings, 1920

Of Gold and Brass

———⟨⟩———

Rings of hearts
filled the air,
filed down to gold
for Il Duce's pile.

Tears of patriotism
allowed
their weight an ache
to the soul.

Crosses cross
the ocean
melted memories of
enduring love.

A list   nine lines
took flight from grandmom's house
eighteen carats crammed Mussolini's coffers
just fine.

It took real brass
for a Fascist
to scoundrel
their legacy.

Grandmom's Iron

It's on the floor by the front door, not there as a prominent door stop. It's there as a reminder of what daily strength I might need. Its resting stand, its perfect mate, reminds me to think before proceeding for any steam that might build up within me; right or wrong, lazy, purposeful, defensive, or offensive.

This iron *is* Grandmom Arcidiacono; small, sturdy, driven, and determined to smooth out any wrinkles which might have befallen her. The curved wooden handle is hand-worn and smooth, its dark bark striated in lines of light browns from the sweat and the pressure of hands once at work. Its oval iron stand is footed with a small metal stopper. Across the top of this stand are the words *Humphries Cast Iron.* Across the bottom, *General Specialty Company.* The inner section of the stand is cut with the letters *H2H* in the center, each letter and number encircled. It could stand alone as a branding iron without a rod; the cut-out design around it was simple, a stained-glass design, no doubt to disperse the iron's heat.

A round wooden knob sits in the middle on top of the iron, the plug for hot water needed for the task. Not merely hot water; scalding, boiling, kids-not-allowed-to-watch liquid. Dangerous even for the steady of hand and for the mature only.

Grandmom's ironing ritual and her duet with her sewing machine are my earliest memories of her. Me on tiptoe, watching from a distance, her pouring seething water into the iron's narrow well, twisting the knob to trap the steam, the metal *clink* each time she set the iron in its resting plate. When one iron lost its heat, a second one (now my sister's) was at the ready. No wrinkle escaped her.

Grandmom was an ironing smith. The tool of her trade on my living room floor was an exultation of manual labor. We are united by wrinkles made straight on cloth and paper.

Grandpop's Rocker

———⋅❦⋅———

Grandpop's rocker lived with us when he moved in, but I don't remember where it was in his house. It's possible it was purchased upon the move for him to have a unique chair of his own.

This chair is an absolute grandpop chair, with no feminine carvings or color shade to suggest female ownership. Grandpop and the chair were made for each other. We placed it in our living room to the left of the foyer entrance. It was the best seat in the house. He could glance out the front storm door, feel the spring and summer breeze, and watch TV without obstruction. None of us sat in his chair. He would rock in a slow rhythm when he smoked his cigars, a vision of contentment. My sister took a picture of him holding one of his great-grandchildren— a moment of his leaning down to kiss her one-year-old forehead. The First Pennsylvania Bank selected this photo for their employee calendar, published in 1980. He died in 1979. This picture is most likely the last one taken of him.

Grandpop willed his rocking chair to me. I never noticed until my husband and I moved into our first home that the ends of the armrests were a different color. Lighter? Grainier? A closer look revealed tiny lines, broken and continuous, a wearing of wood. I visualized him in this chair and recalled his body posture. I realized these were the places where his hands rested. Hands of earth. Sturdy. Completely encasing the chair's arm ends. His sweat, his pulse, his presence in those minute lines that made the wood appear faded. I sat there that first time, my hands over his handiwork, and felt his peace, his presence. I lifted my hands to my face and inhaled the memory of his earthen hands.

Before he died, grandpop gave mom one hundred dollars for Ken and me as a wedding gift. Without debate or hesitation, we bought a smaller rocking chair and a white soup tureen. I imagine him laughing and saying *Something-a to rest-a your feet, and something-a for what you will eat.*

Grandpop's Wine Bottle

———∽◉◉◉∽———

One of the few items unique to grandpop is the wine decanter that lives in my dining room breakfront. I have no living memory without its presence. Ornate enough to be classy, an item set apart in its sole function, perhaps better viewed as a metaphor.

This wine bottle smiled every time grandpop touched it, whether to pour its contents or refill it with the blessings of our labor. Scarcely large enough to hold a gallon but more than enough to unite us. I still picture a favorite photo someone took of grandpop dispensing the sacred drink from this sacred vessel. A fall vintage, most certainly; he's wearing a dark plaid shirt. Grandpop is smiling from ear to ear, his elbow poised in a master-pouring pose. A memory of the wine's bouquet reflecting from the sides of the snapshot.

No one knows what happened to the glass stopper. It was shaped like a lit candle, balanced like a ballet slipper en pointe. I know the bottle was stopper-less when grandpop moved in with us in 1975. Grandpop never openly lamented it; it was never a topic of conversation. He seemed at peace that it survived three generations of children and a lifetime of family gatherings.

Dish detergent ventured not down the neck of this glassware. Such an act would be one of desecration. Cleansed by clear water, nothing else. Over time, the glass turned slightly purple—a royal-like tinge. No doubt exists in my mind that those years of fermentation embedded themselves into this decanter long after the wine presses stopped. I cannot bring my-self to refill this precious object lest a minute speck of grandpop should disappear.

Gravy Pot

———⟨∘⟩———

It must be in our Italian DNA that cooking pots and pans stay in the family. I have several passed down from mom. One of them might have been her mother's. It's probably safe to say that certain pots were allocated for certain foods, or that's how I remember it. The ravioli pot is the most prominent in my mind, a steamship for those pillows of delight. A no-nonsense, range-dominating ranger, it parted the stove without the dispute of its more diminished cronies.

Much of my ethnic learning is probably based on a measure of heresy and truth. Someday I hope to meet a certified chef or one of those PBS folks who test kitchenware to ask my essential question:

If one type of food is cooked in one specified pot, does that pot become seasoned by that food?

My family of female-dominated cooks believes it. Watching them in my mind's eye, I see their bustle and chatter, their involuntary movements of pulling specific pots and pans for certain meals, as if by primal osmosis. I, as an observer and eventual participant, followed suit. No questions asked. The wrong pot pulled would bring a visceral hand slap from an elder. The pots and pans, a drum set, their burners percussive to the water/broth boiling, releasing their treasures while keeping their secrets.

I took this for granted until my Polish mother-in-law shared an observation about cooking with Ken and me in the early months of our marriage. She commented that certain foods tasted better when she prepared them in specific pots. It startled me; did those cultural practices *really* carry the weight of truth?

My mind entered a stick-shift stage, a pivot to a way of life that faces near extinction. Did those kitchen combustions create magic, were they leached from the loving hands of my family, from hands to pots and pans that cooked and stood as silent armor?

Kitchen Cathedral

———— ·ᘒᘏᘒ· ————

Grandmom Arci's kitchen was cozy, small, and active. The most impressive object that resided there was the radio. Not one word of English emitted from its cabinetry as I listened back in time for the memory. As a child, I imagined an invisible aerial directly connected to Italy.

This audio wonder was as elegant and as beautiful as the sounds it released. Made of cherry wood, walnut wood, and cherry veneer, it was round-arched at the top, about four feet in height, with a lattice patterned design on the front. Faux columns lined each side; three round black dials formed a warm triangle in the center. It still reminds me of a door to a huge old church. Its carved steps at its base, the stairway of the sound. One of my greatest regrets was that it was left behind when they sold the house.

Radio Italia was the name of the station, as I recall. The Marconi Miracle glowed through the wood, most frequently Italian opera. Grandmom's voice matched the singing of the soloists, kitchen reformed into a sacred cathedral of Rossini, Leoncavallo, and Mascagni. Grandmom's face became a visage transformed, her dishrag an elegant silk shawl, in a poignant duet with the voices across the sea.

Grandmom's romantic heart made room for the Italian soap opera broadcasts. *Silenzio!* she would warn. We fidgeted while she sat on the edge of a kitchen chair, leaning forward from her waist, her face absorbed in every word and nuance. Grandmom sang the theme songs, snippets of opera, always note for note. Sometimes, she clucked in agreement with the voices. Sometimes, she leaned back and laughed. Sometimes, she would scowl in disapproval. Once I asked her why she frowned during a broadcast. *Leenda, it-sa not-a for you to hear*, was her answer.

Little Boot Knickknack

———⚬⊙⊙⚬———

Very little from Grandmom Arci's house survives. Sometime between her death and grandpop's moving to our house, one of her kitchen knickknacks hitched a ride with his belongings. It was a ceramic boot, four inches wide by five inches high, beige and tan, bottom sole outlined in black, a little green door painted on one side, small red windows shuttered in green on either side. It resembles a shoe with a semblance of a house in its design. The roof, open and peaked, was the home of the soil for a small plant that constantly dwelled there. A red and yellow rooster perches at the top of the boot, green feathers in a display; he seems about to crow. Shoelaces in four eyeholes are behind it. A very compact, whimsical piece, with no year of creation indicated on its sole, only faded letters, that could be *TOA. Made in Japan,* clearly noted. It still brings to mind the nursery rhyme "There was an Old Woman Who Lived in a Shoe."

This knickknack planter lived in grandmom's kitchen near the windowsill. Many seeds or plant cuttings began their life inside this container. Mom followed suit when the shoe relocated to our kitchen. Recently unearthed from mom's belongings, the planter vacant and intact, my find sits in our planter's window awaiting its new lodger. The rooster is still poised for a song, reminding me of grandmom's words *Leenda, always keep a singing bird in your heart.*

Scissors

The pair of scissors found me after Grandmom Arci died, after visiting her home for the last time. It resided inside her scissor holder, the white porcelain-covered footed bowl with the dainty pink flowers. The container had a hole in the center. Odd, the scissors were set inside the bowl, not placed inside the hole, their designated spot.

This little tool fits perfectly in the palm of my hand. Small, black, sturdy, with a tiny black screw in the center, a linchpin keeping the blades in place. Resolute, so much like grandmom.

This instrument sat in my hand as a queen does on a throne. Always an old-world feel to the touch, a distant air of craftswoman ship surrounded it. Remnants of her sweat, salty, buried deep within its edges. Clasped in her young girl Anna's hand, it crossed the ocean with her. This royal tool of her trade held her heart, work, sorrows, and dreams. Hand and scissors together guided angles and cuts of hand-drawn patterns and cloth to perfection. Cutting what needed to be free, cutting the knotted ends that bound her new creations.

The sure sign of death was grandmom's motionless hands in the coffin; the only time I did not see them moving. Survived by her scissors, they mourned her. It went underground, placed itself inside the covered dish, its resting place inside it, invisible under the hole.

When the scissors found me, its release was bittersweet. My astonished gasp breathed over the century-old marker. My hand trembled, and a blanket closed over this pair. I brought it to my heart, swayed in silence, a new ship sailing.

Etruscan Charioteer

Some objects speak to you. My husband Ken found a bronze Etruscan charioteer from somewhere long forgotten. Very sparse, posture very straight, a figure one might see in an artifacts exhibit. It is a strange green-bronze color. Too rustic to shine up. Its wheels are motionless, but my mind keeps turning whenever I look at it. It would be so easy to deem this statue primitive in appearance. I understand that these works of art are far more brilliant; their execution was probably far more complex, perhaps more meaningful.

Imagine this as a gift for a job well done, an emblem of strength, perhaps the story of one of my ancestors, a forefather, possibly striving to be human.

Downstairs, Upstairs, Outside

───⌘───

The spirits of two old friends unexpectedly cross paths. Primo, the wine press, and The Iron Matron meet in front of the house they still claim as theirs. They speak slowly, almost unaware of the other. Their sketchy English necessitates the narrative powers of the house's marble stoop, Carrara. They defer to her telling with an Italian word or two or a slip in syntax.

The marble steps begin with the Italian expression:

Buon vino fa buon sangue.
(Good wine makes good blood.)

Carrara continues: the basement smells of secrets. Primo knows them all, and he wants to share one with you. He says: most of the year, I live in semi-darkness, well cared for in this loving home by Gaetano, Sebastiana (Anna), and the family. So well cared for, before and after every October.

Every October, we make wine in my basement, the date not set in stone but in grapes. I, the primo wine press; my eyes blink as Gaetano removes my linen cover. His heavy footsteps take him outside for the delivery. Our neighbors hide their breath behind lace curtains, expecting signs of the annual event. The produce truck arrives from the Italian market. Grapes in their crates rumble to our little row house on our small street—crates and crates of purple goodness, royal purple beads exposed to the autumn sun, regal Zinfandel. Their—*how you say it*—"less robusto" brothers, Moscato green grapes. The rumble signals nonfamily to their doorways. They decide to go outside, pretending to sweep their sidewalks, pretending not to eye "Tanno," hoping he approaches them with clusters of Nature's pearls, counting on his generosity. They smile— *Grazie!* (Thank you!)

My spot needs no preparation. All is ready for the purple heart of our ritual. The family is here, split in two—women upstairs to cook; men and grandchildren downstairs with me. With our smaller presses, I'm trying to remember how many (Counting: *Uno . . . due . . . tre . . . quattro . . .*) and the number of wooden casks. Our secret recipe holds tight within these sacred barrels. The grandchildren stand waiting on the stairway. Waiting. All but one. She was too big to stand on a small step with many cousins. Leenda. Too excited. No *pazienza* (patience). Too clumsy.

The recipe—simple:

1. Zinfandel and Moscato—per batch.
2. Three crates of "Z" red grapes.
3. One crate of "M" white grapes.

My *padrones* toss the fruit inside me, one batch at a time. Each time, they stuff me like a Thanksgiving turkey: over and over: colors of red, plum, light green, soft purple. Grapes go in; grape gravy comes out.

The pull of my long iron lever at the top sets the process in motion— squish, Squish, SQUISH!!! The Bacchus juice runs out of the press to the gully at the bottom of my barrel. The men stand in line to catch the flow in buckets and fill the casks. They plug them and mark the date on each barrel. Time does the rest. *Pazienza!*

Gaetano lines up his restless grandchildren, Leenda, the strongest one, at my lever's end, him beside her. Many little hands on my arm. Gaetano counts, *uno, duo, tre,* and pulls too quickly. Leenda falls backward; cousins knock on top of her to the floor. A wobbly purple stream hisses through me. My lever pitches backward—*a-pazzo* (crazy). A crazy motion.

Leenda cannot stand up. The cellar walls keep moving. Leenda falls again, laughing, breathing in more wined air. Gaetano guides her to the basement landing. He tells her not to move without him. His eyes say, *"Grandmom will **kill** me if she sees you like this!"*

My departure? Still there, I think. One of my grandsons, Terzo, lives with Leenda. She rescues him from the careless hands of a relative who left him outside. Leenda will repair him; the center spindle is still there. She'll turn him into an Italian herb planter with ivy winding around that middle shaft.

Carrara and the wine press Primo laugh. A breeze floats between these spirits.

∿⤳◯◟∿

Carrara continues with the story of the second soul. She hears her sigh. Carrara and The Iron Matron tell her story together.

Leenda's sister accidentally smothers me, Anna's iron, The Iron Matron, under a pile of clothes after their mother, Mary, Gaetano's daughter, moves in with her. She moves me to the second floor as her bedroom doorstop. Acrophobia grips me. Leenda rescues me when her sister finds my twin in her basement.

Leenda is a strange grandchild who follows her grandparents everywhere, especially Anna. Perhaps it's because only Leenda is allowed to iron with her. No one raises a stink about helping when they see their grandmother remove the ironing board from the kitchen closet. They want to jump rope in the backyard; they wait until the clothes disappear from the clothesline. Anna gathers the laundry from the sun's starching, stacks it like paper soldiers on the kitchen table, and places Gaetano's white Sunday shirts on the top of the pile. Curtains follow separately. Anna habitually removes laundry from its hung position—less wrinkles, less worry!

These clean-smelling martyrs, in their colors, meet their doom once I am prepared. Water hisses on the stove in the large black pot, boiling without mercy, soon to gurgle down the shaft to my belly, the metal oppressor. Leenda needs no warning; she waits, seated until called. I trust Anna's skills. She funnels the nearly scalding water into the tiny hole in the center of my metal pyramid, soon to part their wrinkles. Anna twists the screw-like knob over the hole, captures water massages, and saunas my interior.

People think we old iron matrons are Satan's handbags. But there is another job that eases our harshness, for laundry ironed later, the sprinkling of linen.

It works like this:

1. Laundry-in-waiting is evenly water-moistened by a sprinkler-capped shaker.
2. Each item is rolled like a sausage.
3. Each item is placed in a plastic bag, as many as possible.
4. Each bag is stored far back in the refrigerator for future pressings.

A safe spot for clothing as tight as corsets. They await removal, my rubbing heat against their coldness a relief. This is Leenda's favorite task. I teach generations this preparation ritual.

Leenda relieves me from that spot of loneliness. Our gazes meet sometimes; no more am I a threat of steamy revenge. Leenda's desire to be by our side still connects us with Anna. Hard labor moments bond us forever.

My new world is Leenda's front door stop. I feel the weather from the ins and outs of each day. As the iron valet, I hear lawnmowers whine, dogs bark, and packages thump on the porch. Anna's hand sweat lines still trace my handle, tracks of the death of her female infant, worry when she carried twins she nearly aborted, one of them Leenda's mother. Of the Great Depression and World War II. Leenda touches my handle, my knowledge. My bottom surface is still smooth. She places me on my "rest friend," H2H, her grace under my pressure. Sometimes, Leenda rubs me, smiles, still pretends I'm Aladdin's lamp. She rubs me for Anna Aladdin to appear and wishes for one more ironing task and lever pull.

Carrara falls silent. Primo and Iron Matron look like they are waiting for her to speak. She raises her head and tells her own story.

∾⚬Ꙩ⚬∾

I exist in the background, but I'm really in front of everything. I learn English from the sidewalk up:

> I learn from the morning sun
> when the milkman's bottles clink
> against the top level of my waiting stoop
>
> I learn from all the children
> playing ball in the narrow street
> small street, their voices bouncing   high
>
> I learn of the world beyond,
> of all of it, the war, the Influenza
> of the neighbors bringing out their dead
>
> I learn when each night falls
> when lovers whisper arm in arm
> while mothers call their children in to sleep.

No one neglects me or takes me for granted. There is a ritual for me, too, every Saturday morning. Every day before Sunday, the ladies make a clean sweep and scrub my white stone. The soapy water bathes my spirit to its luster, shining under my cold surface. There is that day in early October when Gaetano's and Anna's daughter joins the women in their weekly task. Like always. But this day is not like the other "always." It is her wedding day—white dress, white veil, white shoes to follow later.

Leenda to follow soon after.

Behind the Ironed Curtain

—◦⟨⟨⟩⟩◦—

The water hissed on the stove in the Vulcan black pot, boiling without mercy, soon to gurgle down the shaft to the belly of the iron, the metal oppressor of oppressors. I needed no warning to remain seated until called to assist. It terrified and eluded me how Grandmom funneled the nearly scalding water into the microscopic hole in the center of the metal pyramid, soon to part wrinkles as Moses did to the Red Sea. She twisted the screw-shaped nob over the hole to entrap the steam.

In their colors and hues, the clean-smelling martyrs would meet their doom once the iron was prepared. Grandmom retrieved the laundry from the starching of the sun, laundry stacked like paper soldiers, Grandpop's white Sunday shirt positioned at the apex. Kitchen and living room curtains followed in their separate, sanctified group, first in the lineup for prime arm and iron attention. One never removed laundry without doing so from its hung position on the clothesline; it kept wrinkles at bay. This practice brought relief to the ironer and the fabric.

The clink of the iron on its resting plate was the only object that could withstand its heat. Even that was short-lived. Italian opera floated over us in counterpoint from the radio safely perched atop the refrigerator, music doth soothe the savage pile, near cringing in waiting.

The technique of the task made all the difference. The art of heat distribution was an admired, sought-after skill. Pressure too light and a waste of heat and steam would befall the sacrificial fabric. Too heavy or too long applied meant certain scorching or ruination of the article flanked on the ironing board, with certain scorching glances from Grandmom to follow. That was enough to dampen any active volunteering from the upcoming generation.

The chore of laundering and ironing preempted any other routine activity at Grandmom's house. The sterile process left no room for the ethnic aroma of her cooking. The process commanded that process and only that process.

Yet, the most intriguing activity associated with that Satan's handbag of an iron centered on the sprinkling rite of linen. When laundry-in-waiting needed postponing for ironing, sprinkling, and rolling were substituted. Each piece of clothing was gently and evenly sprinkled with water from a cylindrical shaker with holes poked into its cap. Each item was rolled very tightly, placed in a bag like sausages in casings, and stored at the back of the refrigerator for future pressings. Grandmom, Mom, and every woman I knew as a child followed this practice. A designated refrigerator drawer was also a prime location. This designated drawer meant sole sanctuary, apparel tight as strait-laced corsets spooned together for maximum conformity and crispness. Once retrieved and opened for ironing, linens and attire unwrapped themselves gratefully for the presence of the iron's massaging heat, the process far quicker and more effective. That was my favorite task.

One day, Grandmom caught me rubbing the iron surface in a rare, cold moment. I disarmed her by explaining I was rubbing Aladdin's Lamp. I thought it was about time he emerged from his metal haven and helped us.

My relieving grandmom's iron from its recent post at my sister's house was deserving. We need to reconnect on common ground. I want to meet its gaze, no more a threat of steamy vengeance but an emblem of our relationship. Those moments of shared hard labor were among the few rare endeavors with a common goal that united my grandmom and me. For all her lack of formal education, this task, and my desire to be by her side, made me her obvious second-generation successor, following her daughter as the Ironing Maiden-in-Waiting.

Before I placed it in its new home, I put my hand on the handle, smoothed by her determined strength and skill, convinced I could feel the imprint of her hand along the grain of the wooden handle, longing to absorb some of her trapped sweat buried beneath its surface. I was bound to "Aladdin rub" the iron again. I wished for her, Sebastiana, my Aladdin, to appear. I wished for that time back when I loved ironing.

It seems I was the only granddaughter who ironed with Grandmom. It was such a pleasure to be allowed to help from the moment she removed the ironing board from the kitchen closet. I could hardly wait to help her de-flag the clothes from the clothesline.

In certain circles through the years, whenever someone mentions the sprinkling of linen for ironing, the demarcation line appears like a laser beam. The phrase either conjures immediate recognition or total puzzlement. Laughter invariably follows, as do occasional confessions from those of us who still honor this practice.

I wish for that time back when I loved ironing with Grandmom.

Burnt Offerings

———————

In Grandmom Arci's house of endless scents, secured in a furtive spot, is a hidden box of aging wrappers, round banded, for the moment of silent pleasure. Slowly processed cylinders of burnt sienna cigars, wrapped and packed by burnt sienna hands, await their master.

Grandmom upheld her daily vigil at Church. Grandpop retrieved his stash in her absence. Grandmom lit white votive candles surrounding the Blessed Virgin Mary statue. Grandpop, in the house vestibule, vestibule door closed, front door open, illuminated his serene space with his *Nicotiana tabacum*, his corona, his cigar.

Each to their sanctum sanctorum, each to their Solomonic columns of smoke, burnt wax, and burnt sienna ash. Wax-dripped fingers and cherry-flavored fingernails. Deep thoughts, deep prayers, deep inhaling. A ceaseless entreaty of Grandmom's prayers to Heaven for Grandpop's smoking to cease. Grandpop's guilty pleasure for his next indrawn breath of raw, earthy tobacco: of peace, of solitude, of Sicily. Their separate vespers to the same God.

Our house inherits the scent of those raw and burnt brownish embers when Grandpop resided with us for the last four years of his life. The rocking chair in the living room was his throne. The front door, screen down, the burnt sienna cigar incensing the air as it hallowed the walls and the welcome mat. The El Producto, Phillies Titan, and Europa brands his smoking Magi.

When there was no scent of sienna in our house that first Christmas, the walls dimmed by its absence. I wandered, aimless and bereft, through every room. The holiday decorations, my mother's attempt to honor her father's love of the season, did not console me. I stumbled in grief, breathing for that missing fragrance. For reasons unknown, I stopped before the cedar closet. I twisted the doorknob, this act unconscious, offhand. The door opened.

The shock of recognition hit me full force as I glance up. On the top shelf were the Cigar Tobacco Magi boxes: the El Producto, the Phillies Titan, and the Europa. Empty of their original contents, they were now ribbon-bound, hidden during another era. Love letters, those ancient dreams, cherry burnt sienna aroma released to the air, ingrained into the heart of these sacred vessels, set free for one joyous inhaling. My chest embraced the boxes; I, a mother reluctant to send her child into the world.

It didn't all go up in smoke after all.

Seal of Approval

———◦⊙◦———

Holiday attire was always subject to Grandmom Arci's approval, especially during Easter. Grandmom was the consummate seamstress; she held my mother hostage in her assessment of her clothing choices throughout her life. It extended to her grandchildren's apparel. Her only daughter endured scrutiny; grandmom's sons and their children were not considered with the same dissection. That was for their wives to handle.

Grandmom's inspection was atypical, even for an Italian lady. Hers was a bottom-up approach. Shoes first. Shoes were body language, grandmom's eyes alert in their roundabout perusal, her furtive sniff for shoe polish or hand-me-downs. Socks, like soldiers, must be straight in pattern alignment. Mom tolerated this ritual and relinquished any disputes. Grandmom's nod meant we passed muster, save for some minute detail correctable before a Big Day. My disconcertedness met me at grandmom's impressive, spotless, white marble front steps. Climbing those four Everest blocks with dress shoes was adeptness in motion. One foot dragged movement could portent certain scuff marks, shoe wreckage that would not escape her notice. Passing the white dress shoe inspection was a pinnacle of relief.

Once, when grandmom caught me in an eye-roll over her fussiness, she firmly grabbed my arm and said, *Leenda, what-a good-a is it-a to be all dressed up-a, if you wear-a old, broken, dirty shoes?*

Whenever I glance down at my feet in a final survey of apparel, my soul still searches for her final seal of approval.

Angel of Peace

———⟨⟩———

Grandpop had a standing rule: No talking permitted during dinner.

This directive is something utterly foreign to Italian protocol. Dinner scenes of the ethnic group most often depicted in movies/TV/commercials are Italian meals. Scenes bursting with food, drink, laughter, teasing, incessant cross conversations, and hand signals. No chair is ever still for long.

But dinner at the Arcidiacono house was different. Grandpop Arci worked in a textile mill. Roaring looms, shuttles, carts, and yelling of supervisors dinned his ears incessantly for decades. The squeak of trolley wheels and the automobile introduction, which he called *The Machine*, added to the clamor of his every waking moment.

We dined as if we were in church; it was ironic that church was the last place on earth grandpop wanted to be. So, quiet it had to be. Grandpop would state, when he sat at the table, that the Angel of Peace was present. He wanted no less than peace and quiet. The only sound was silverware touching the plates.

For us kids, and me in particular, this was torment. I would twist the tablecloth and try to touch my foot to my mother's leg under the table to get her attention. My father would settle every squirmy moment with "The Look," that glance that all Italian men inherit in utero. We could clamor to our heart's content when it was time for dessert, but time stood still as we waited for that movement grandpop would make with his arm signaling the silence to end.

As time passed and we grew older, grandpop relaxed the rule. The slight deafness he acquired from those aural assaults lessened his perception of the noise level. In his advanced age, he devised a prayer that he'd whisper to my mother at every meal, *Posso godermi questo e avere spazio per il prossimo pasto.* May I enjoy this and have room for the next meal.

Scentventures in Aroma Land

—◦◦◦—

Wine-scented basement walls,
Italian cookies in wedding halls,
boiled oil for shells, cannoli filling,
every bite so tasty, so thrilling,
ravioli rising to the top of the pot,
simmering gravy hits the spot!
Peppers and eggs dance in the skillet:
oregano, garlic, parsley to fill it.
Pinching basil to release
fragrance that will never cease.
Grated Locatelli cheese,
baked biscotti fills the breeze.
Vinegar is not neglected,
adding zest to greens rejected.
Coffee hot greetings, raw meat in pans,
Home far away in the palm of their hands.

Omerta

—❦—

Both sets of grandparents never spoke of the Mafia. Grandpop Arci was adamant about it: no jokes, no books, no movies, no TV shows. No hint of the word permitted. Any misbehavior never met with threats that the Mafia might appear to punish us.

I knew one thing and surmised the other. Someone approached grandpop Arci when he was a young man to join the *Cosa Nostra*, our thing. Grandpop refused; he had a young family, he told the person he could not read or write (he read the newspaper, *Il Popolo Italiano*), and his English was *not-a so good*. No one approached him after this conversation.

I surmise grandpop witnessed the Mafia in action in Sicily and wanted no part of it. He was a soft-spoken man who lived a temperate life and never raised a hand to his family. All he needed to do to keep us in line was give us "The Look." That calm, inscrutable stare signaled you were in trouble—that silence.

Omerta. Silence.

The Sacred Heart

Valentine's Day
thanksgiving of the heart
thanksgiving for the heart

He brought the box
of chocolates
no thought of weather
they had been together
since forever

That last heart
unknown to us.
Red velvet love
Red velvet bow

Grandpop,
You wore your heart
for her
on your sleeve
in hand the box
beat your love.

The nurses smiled
some of them sighed
Two days later
Grandmom died.
You   in 1979

Your sacred hearts
Together

Forever.

Opera Verismo

———⟨∘⟩———

(Involving Everyday Characters)

PRELUDE: *Parkinson's Disease is a disorder of the central nervous system. Hand tremors are the usual symptom. A progressive disease, onset mostly mild. Nerve cell damage causes dopamine levels to drop. Typically, expressed in five stages. It affects the tempo of everyday life. Tempo, in the anatomy of opera, controls the music's momentum.*

Grandmom's hands are always moving. She is stitching, drawing patterns, ironing, and threading needles. She is singing all the while. I observe and learn by osmosis; her natural abilities flow from her hands to mine. I grasp no clue of the wispy shake of her right hand on that airy day.

ANDANTE (LEISURELY PACE): SCENE 1: *Mild symptoms, daily activities unencumbered. Posture and facial expressions change. Tremors may appear on one side of the body.*

Grandmom's hands continue their daily living journey, albeit she favors her left hand. The shift to the left went unnoticed. Her singing is seamless, her voice smiling, her closed eyes scoring each note. Each stitch is a song-beat. She sews, and she sings the aria "Vesti la Giubba" from Leoncavallo's opera "Pagliacci" (The Clowns). The story of Canio, the tragic clown. She's an angelic soprano, a tessitura, a High C vocalist of the highest timbre, a sanctuary of sound.

Singing is more complex than speech, demanding more from the larynx, breath, vocal cords, and throat muscles. Parkinson's creates a tug of war among these singing parts, notes diminishing their ability to sustain melodious sound, desperate in locked combat with breath control, pitch control, and throat muscles.

ACCELERANDO (SPEEDING UP): SCENE 2: *Tremor and rigidity can manifest on both sides of the body. Walking, posture, and daily tasks become difficult.*

Grandmom's mind-over-brain matter leads her hands, but her mental arm wrestling is starting to lose its grip. Her singing, now adagio, is off tempo. Perhaps she knows; perhaps her mind provides the sounds she can no longer make.

ALLARGANDO (GROWING BROADER): SCENE 3: *Mid-stage disease, loss of balance, slow movements.*

Grandmom's unerring talent of threading a needle without looking falters. I watch as her attempts fail. She purses her lips, hums to herself, and tries again, full focus on the slender filament that refuses to pass through the elongated hole. I stand behind her to keep her steady. We thread the needle together with her atonic and my abiding hands in a guided duet. Grandmom leans back, her coiled, braided hair with a frustrated scent of sweat and a halo imprinting my tee shirt.

She sings the aria again from "Pagliacci."

The literal meaning of "Vesti La Giubba" is "put on the costume." Canio learns his spouse is unfaithful as he prepares for his clown performance. He sings of this betrayal. Grief is protracted; he puts on the costume. The show must go on.

Grandmom continues to sing, and the notes slip slide. I am silent; she does not feel me cry.

INTERVALLO (INTERMISSION): *Levodopa (L-dopa), a central nervous system agent, is developed in the late 1960s. This amino acid converts to dopamine in the substantia nigra region of the brain, the nucleus of the midbrain. It reduces stiffness and tremors and enhances muscle control.*

Grandmom's hands rebound, rebound with this "miracle drug." Her almost-self returns. Her mind is suspicious; she takes no movements for granted. I keep my hands to myself. Her solo performance of threading the needle sets her near the High C range again.

Together, we hum the iconic, wordless "Intermezzo" from Mascagni's opera "Cavalleria Rusticana," the story of rustic Sicilian chivalry. We hum its slow, cherished, longing rhythm. The contemplation of melancholic solitude. The radio, a cathedral-arched design, an elegant accompaniment, our trio of sound. Grandmom's ethereal soprano overtone and my hushed alto undertone a heartfelt caress.

MENO MOSSO (LESS MOVEMENT, SLOWER): SCENE 4: *Symptoms become severe and limiting.*

Grandmom's reprieve is short-lived. We rejoice in that reprieve. For a fleeting moment, L-dopa grants us our final concert with her Singer sewing machine. Grandmom cranks the wheel and guides the fabric under the needle's pressure foot. My feet seesaw the foot pedal tray at her feet, as I once did by hand as a child crawling under the machine's cabinet. Perhaps she sing-songs my name haltingly, "Leenda, Leenda."

APPENATO (EXHIBITING SUFFERING): SCENE 5: *Most debilitating stage. Stiffness, hallucinations, and delusions.*

Grandmom's suffering intensifies, suffering cut short miraculously by another complication. A stomach tumor. Her tumor demands immediate surgery. Her hands wave danger signs at me when I visit her in the hospital. She shrieks and wails in Italian that *L'uomone a cavallo*, the man on the horse, is coming for her. Her hands thrust upward to push me away.

"Leenda, Leenda! He comes for me!! Leave before he takes you too!!!" Parkinson's ravages her beautiful voice, and lamenting sounds trail after me as I stumble into the corridor.

Grandmom dies three days later.

ADDOLORATO (GRIEF): ENCORE

I begin to understand that people die *with* Parkinson's Disease, not *of* it.

I begin to understand that the Italian legend of "The Man on the Horse" as the harbinger of Death is real. Grandmom pushed me away from her just in time.

When I walk to her coffin and see her hands for the last time, it is the only time I do not see them moving.

Grandmom Arci sewing.

Parting Words

———◦◦◦———

The old Italian man knew he was dying. All the signs were there. He knew it. The family knew it. Agitation can be part of the death process, but his anxiety was not that kind of distress. His was not death restlessness but a disquiet, an internal mental struggle, soon to slip from his grasp. He was never so serious or intent; this moment was never so important to him.

His vigilant daughter whispered, *Pop, what's wrong?* He reached for her hand, trembling. She thought he was afraid until he spoke these words:

When your mother was pregnant with you and your brother, she was afraid. I was afraid. Things were so bad for us. I went to the pharmacista man at the drugstore. He told us not to do anything, not to do anything to harm you.

His daughter could not comprehend his words. His eyes shone with tears. He continued, *If we had done what we were thinking to do, where would I be now? Who would have taken care of your mother and me?*

In his lifetime, the old gentleman's idea of faith and churchgoing gravitated to smoking cigars in his backyard and vestibule. But Grand-pop Arci knew what he was facing, and he sought a final confession. When he knew his daughter understood, he slipped into absolution.

His daughter told her oldest daughter toward the end of her days; she made her swear not to reveal this exchange until her passing.

Where would I be now? Where would I be now, her oldest child?

Realization of Family of Origin

———•◦◦◦•———

It was a great surprise to me to learn that my father's parents were not born in Italy. I took it for granted. My mother's parents came from Sicily, *the other side*, they'd always said. Rose (Lauria) Marrone and Raffaele (Ralph) Marrone were six years younger than my maternal grandfather. That aside, their cultural practices, world views, speech patterns, and non-verbal communication were as solidly ethnic as anyone from any part of Italy or Sicily. They settled in the Bella Vista section of South Philadelphia, the corner property of 7th and Montrose Streets, two blocks away from the Italian Market. Three of their four children were born in this house. My father always joked that he was never born because there was no birth certificate to attest to his humanity. My aunt died in this house; her wish was to depart the earth from where she arrived. My cousin, her daughter, still lives there.

The house is at the end of a narrow street. St. Mary Magdalen de Pazzi Church, the oldest Italian Catholic parish in the United States, is across the street, in the middle of the block. Today's presence of cars and condominiums significantly narrows the neighborhood's width. With its high-pitched steps at the entrance, this beautiful place is still a vision of elegant architectural wonder. My father's family maintained a deep devotion to the church and all matters of the Italian way. Fervor ran high among parishioners in those early days, enforced from the moment of an infant's first breath.

Parents who named children after saints was second only to naming a child after a parent or grandparent. In those days, South Philadelphian parents seemed to promise that one of their daughters must be named Rita, in some manner, after Saint Rita of Cascia, Rome. The patroness of the Impossible. One of my father's sisters was named Rita. My mother's middle name was Rita. St. Rita's national shrine is on Broad Street. Her following remains faithful and intense.

St. Mary Magdalen parish held majestic feast day celebrations. My grandmother and father often noted the favorites besides Mary Magdalen: the Blessed Virgin Mary, St. Rita, St. Rocco. The highly decorated statue of the feast day saint would be carried on a raised platform by any non-disabled young boy or man, six or eight to a platform. The street was clogged with devoted parishioners pressing petitions and coins upon the carved image of their favorite saint, supported by its manpowered, elevated dais. A procession was followed by singing, praying, and music. The practice continues to this day; other Italian parishes nearby still maintain the tradition.

My father's family was always involved in these events, a complete demonstration of Italian faith in action. My father was a parish altar boy for many years. The parish was knit even closer to religion and culture by the talent of a young man who lived around the corner from my family. He was Mario Lanza, considered the most outstanding opera tenor of the twentieth century, still revered by the remembering few of my generation. One Christmas Eve, as a young boy, he sang in the church choir loft. No doubt, upon hearing his voice, the parishioners made the sign of the cross in Italian, rosaries held to their breast, deeming him the reincarnation of the great Enrico Caruso, who died the year Lanza was born in 1921. (The fact that Lanza was born on January 31 and Caruso died on August 2 was immaterial.)

With this closeness came a parochial attitude, not always ecumenical. When the pastor found out my father planned to marry my mother, who was from St. Nicholas of Tolentine Church, a few blocks away, he chided him. *Carmen, what's the matter with you? Couldn't you marry a nice girl from our parish?*

A series of events caused our relationship with my father's parents to vary from my mother's side. Grandpop Marrone died in 1957 of throat cancer. I was four and a half years old. My Uncle Joe, the youngest son, became widowed in 1965 at thirty-three when his spouse died of leukemia. At thirty years of age, Aunt Dot's early demise left three children under seven motherless. At fifty-seven, Grandmom Marrone moved in with Uncle Joe and raised the children until he married several years later.

I could never view my Marrone grandparents as American Italian, their heritage and faith so strongly upheld. The spirit of ethnicity dominated and permeated their lives and their offspring. Their four children married Italians who resided in the area. The bond of their cultural background will always remain as vital to me as my Arcidiacono grandparents.

Linda with paternal grandparents, Ralph and Rose Marrone, 1954

Surname Survival

※

My maiden surname survived to Marrone after two prior inter-
ventions of fate. Upon my father's family's arrival to America,
their surname, Maurone (or Mauroni?), became Marrone.

When my Grandpop Marrone was a young man, hiring an Italian for
any job outside his South Philadelphia vicinity was anathema. He and
my grandmother lived in the Buena Vista section, heavily Italian, two
blocks from the Italian Market. Changing the spelling of his last name
to *Morrone* gave it an Irish twist, with an aural "y" added unconsciously
by his inflection. Numerous family members followed his example and
never reclaimed the original spelling.

Grandpop Marrone, tall, handsome, fair-skinned, fair-haired, and
blue-eyed, was often called "The Irish Cop." I cannot say his surname's
spelling came into question, but I know he worked for a while for John
B. Kelly Sr., father of actress and princess Grace Kelly. Mr. Kelly made
his fortune in bricklaying and construction. Grandmom Marrone told
me stories of Mr. Kelly occasionally stopping by their house. She was
quite fond of him, describing him as *a good man to our family.* I still see
his "Kelly for Brickwood" advertisement in my young mind's eye. Three
words modestly lettered in black on a single red brick. My adult mind
realizes he must have known grandpop's name ruse when he first crossed
the family threshold but never divulged his discovery. Grandmom's sum-
mation of his character protected us.

Christmas Reprise

———⁊ʘɞ·———

Every Christmas, I hear my grandmother's voice.

My maternal grandmother, Sebastiana Arcidiacono, could sing like an angel. Whenever she attended Mass at her Italian parish, St. Nicholas of Tolentine Church on Watkins Street in South Philadelphia, no one needed to wonder who was singing.

The only Christmas carol I remember her singing was "Silent Night." Or, instead, "Sire-ly Night." Her Italian accent made it impossible for her to pronounce many English words correctly. So, "Sire-ly Night" was "Silent Night."

No one could ever sing "Silent Night" the way she could. When I was a child, I begged her to sing it. I'd do it on purpose. Not because I wanted to make fun of her but because her version of the song, with the blended English and Italian words, was so endearing. The sincerity of her feeling, the music, and what it represented compensated for her interpretation. Her soprano voice would fill the small kitchen of her South Philadelphia home, the home I so dearly loved on Fernon Street, creating a Nativity of Sound.

·ᴥɞʘᴥ·

The first Christmas she was gone, it all came back to me. There was that quiet moment, the ethereal pause between wakefulness and sleep, when I heard her sing. That was in 1974. I held this secret for years. Since then, I have experienced this moment every Christmas.

I haven't heard her sing yet this year, but there is still time—a time when I will need to listen to her voice of comfort again. To tell me she is still with me, sleeping in Heavenly Peace.

Buon Natale, Grandmom.

Section II

⮾

ITALIAN – AMERICAN

Bearing Witness

———◦◦◦———

Dad spoke very little of World War II. I imagine the influx of PBS documentaries about the Greatest Generation gave him pause. One night, after viewing one of those presentations, he shared the following story with me:

He was stationed in London, England, serving in the Army in the Intelligence Unit. He was never involved in active combat, but the rattling bombs and the aftershocks of tilting buildings surrounded him. Evening adventures outdoors left nothing for the imagination of soldiers deployed indoors.

One evening, dad ventured outside his illusionary protective domain. It was one of the few nights of quiet that he could recall. The streets were empty and damp from twilight rainfall. A young man approached him. He spoke slowly; dad could hardly hear him. Dad reared his head back when the full intent of the young man's words reached his ears.

Dad forgot I was there. He didn't look at me; it seemed he couldn't. The young man mumbled a few more words, the British accent clearly understood. He repeated what the young man said aloud, in bits and pieces, about his wife *being available; not much was required; they just needed enough to get by.*

Dad glanced over my head; his eyes widened at his unseeable reverie. Was the scene in his mind, or was the actual meaning of the young man's offer finally resonating with what he might not have fully understood until this moment?

Silence fell between us. I did not ask what happened next; Dad offered no confession. But I know what he did. There is no doubt in my mind about what he did. He tucked away that memory, as all war survivors did, tightly as they tucked their daily newspaper under their arms on their way home from work. Mental print, there but rarely seen. He rose from his chair in the living room and walked upstairs.

Army Cot and Needle Book

In the Smithsonian section
of the garage You are there

folded   quiet   ready to release
your collapsed ribs
I stretched you
to the light of day

did you shiver in relief
did you quiver in memory
in the mighty fear
in the thunder of war

did dad entomb himself
in your womb   to seek
your cot cloth comfort?

In a family strongbox
your Army and Navy needlebook.
Needles like soldiers
shiny and straight   silver steel
in rust-proof tissue.

Needle eyes at attention
for thread to pass through
portal to pull the world
hanging
by
   a
       thread
together.

They were ready for a peaceful world
that's not.

Stop, Children!

We had to tiptoe
when Dad slept.
The couch a lyre
for his rest.

The slightest noise
he'd jump the fire—
the couch turned pyre

his eyes ablaze
breath quick
face reddened

We'd scurry from
his Armageddon
out of his sight
til he was   calm.

Years pass   one day,
a loud boom
jolts my nerves:

The War! That's it!
Dad's jolt from sleep
I recollect the sound.

Namesakes

Mom was named for you
the you   she never knew
You, Maria, born a century past.

Always afraid to ask
I wondered   about you
I still do.

First female family child
in their New World.
your world   so brief
the Grief
went far beyond
your seven days
on earth.

There is no photo of you.
My mother took   your place
your name   given to her.

You, lost in the cemetery
of Holy Cross   It holds
your mystery   where
are you   under that earth?

There you were   and are
in mom's name
Here   you are   always
in my heart.
You,   Aunt Maria,   You.

Diptych: Two at Once

―――❦―――

PART 1: LADIES' FIRST

Maria, my mother, was born first. Her father gleefully exclaimed; *This one is mine! This one is Papa's doll-ee!!* Two brothers were born before her, Sebastiano and Franzi, eleven and six years her senior. Her father's words of joy were bittersweet after the loss of a daughter in 1920. She was barely a week old. Her cause of death, pneumonia, was never shared openly with the family. Her name bestowed upon my mother, a dark-haired child, was sweet from the start. My mother grew into a beautiful girl, young woman, spouse, mother, and grandmother. Common sense to the hilt, uncommon loveliness emanated from her, from the inside out. Mom came into the world from a shared womb. She lived her life always sharing with others.

Mom loved butterflies. Yellow was her favorite color. Since her passing in 2016, these flying flowers have visited me often. When I take walks to clear my head, when thoughts furrow inside me and call me to Nature, they are there, these flutter-bys (as my daughter called them when she was a little girl). They are calm in their fluttering; they come close to me, these pale white/pale yellow apparitions.

Perhaps sharing her space from the start made her heart bloom early and let all her goodness out—one of two. Two ova, separate yet together, the "twin word" of their bond.

PART 2: SECOND TO NONE

Grandmom's doctor wasn't sure if she was pregnant with twins. But all the little old Italian ladies in her neighborhood were certain of it. Those little old Italian ladies knew *everything*. They knew that heartburn during pregnancy meant the child would enter the world with a full head of hair, an old wives' tale borne out in countless births. Grandmom knew she was carrying two offspring. Grandmom knew that one of them was a malcontent in utero, knew this from three prior pregnancies. Those prior gestations taught her calm insight.

Vincenzo followed my mother's lead moments after her arrival. He met the world in a fury, vowing never to be second to anyone again, much less to a female. From his birth forward, nothing would ever stand in his way. His brilliant mind steered him to thoughts often not understood by those around him. His gondola basket was his valise for all things wise: pencils, ruler, protractor, compass. This basket landed back in the family when my aunt donated it to our church flea market, and I purchased it with no knowledge that it was his.

One of two, second to none, two ova together, worlds apart in a world together.

Pet and Plate

—◦❀◦—

During the Depression, my grandparents relocated to a family friend's farm in New Jersey. My mother and her twin brother were nearly three years old. The length of their stay there was never discussed. My mother's strongest memory was their playing with the many farm animals surrounding them. She and her brother became exceedingly fond of one of the rabbits. They befriended this creature; mom recalled its downy softness but not its name.

She clearly recalled the night their pet became the main course at dinner. Mom shrieked, cried, and hid in her mother's lap. No full belly could ever console her. Years later, she owned a black sweater with a black rabbit fur collar. She would often relate this story to me as she stroked the fur's softness.

I inherited the sweater. I think of her story every time I wear it.

Saving Dick and Jane

———∽◦⊙◦∽———

When my dad found a first-grade Dick and Jane primer on the steps of our parish church, my love of reading began. That Sunday afternoon, when a summer breeze rustled its upturned pages like peacock plumage, I ran to it. I couldn't have been much older than four years old. As a four-year-old, I was familiar with our informal home library of reading material. But those sources were rhymes and fairy tales that mom read to me. This was different; my first memory of dad and I venturing to read together.

The book's cover held no indication of ownership. Since the church was closed for the day, there was no place to leave Dick and Jane. Dad felt no qualms as he tucked the book under his arm and took my hand in his to head home. Perhaps an unexpected lesson plan came to his mind as he opened the front door. The sizeable electric living room fan greeted us, a respite from the summer heat.

All was quiet in our house. It was a modest home, with a kitchen door separating mom's realm from the living room. While mom busied herself preparing our evening meal and my brother napped, dad and I sat on the couch. He positioned me on his lap.

When mom read to me before bedtime, her voice carried me over pictures and single letters of the alphabet, letters of all shapes and sizes. Dad's approach was different, far more mysterious. With his left arm around my shoulder, while holding the book, and his right hand guiding my fingers over the squiggly-looking lines, our same-shaped fingers moved to each character. I would learn that those squiggly lines meant something. They were not there by chance. The scent of dad's aftershave weaved through my curls. I vaguely recall leaning back to breathe its pleasantness, leaning into his heartbeat through his sweaty T-shirt. It remains my only memory of our physical closeness.

My awareness grew to other types of print material. I grew curious about the daily newspaper that arrived every afternoon, folded like a papoose. Dad and grandpop unfolded this enigma; their hands stretched out its contents until it covered them, faces hidden. The paper rose and fell in slow waves of their patriarchal breathing. A faint swish of dark, lettered paper floated over them as they read from page to page. Except for the kingly Sunday newspaper, which arrived unfolded, the comics peeked to attract attention. I tried to figure out what it was about these contents that caused curiosity, discussion, and laughter. I copied the adult's behavior, wanting to be like the grownups. Sometimes, I would pick up the discards of their readings. I couldn't understand the appeal of crossword puzzles. Why would anyone want to put letters inside empty blocks? Weren't words that made sense side by side enough?

I loved when the mailman delivered items that resembled books but weren't. They were magazines. *The Ladies Home Journal* was mom's favorite. Once it appeared that I could read with assistance, the *Humpty Dumpty* magazine arrived for me. Both magazines had a peculiar scent I grew to love, that of opening something in written form that was brand new and didn't blacken the ends of your fingers the way newsprint did. I loved when Dad would take a few minutes to read my magazine with me if he weren't too tired after coming home from work. The fairy tale readings would come with Mom by my side before I went to sleep for the night.

As I grew older, I came to understand that every Catholic home in the area claimed four revered books: The Bible, the two telephone directories known as the White Pages for residents and the Yellow Pages for business, and the Sears Catalog (aka The Wish Book). Our family bible was sizable, with a red leather cover, gold lettering, and gold edgings on every page, a threatening tome. The White Pages lost its appeal once I found our name and the names of everyone that mattered to me. The Yellow Pages were for grownups when something serious was sought or needed. Those pages held no intrigue for me. I found a personal practical use for these great cornerstones, that of adding climbing height to a kitchen chair to snag a treat from the cookie jar that teased me from the top of the refrigerator. Books really can teach you to achieve anything one's heart desires.

That was the first lesson I learned from my father.

Palmistry and Ponytails

It's Palm Sunday again. As a kid in South Philadelphia, I remember seeing ornate palm-woven arrangements on doorways, in windows, and in gardens. Arrangements made by hand, made from the palms, were distributed to the parishioners during Palm Sunday Mass.

Dad was an expert palm weaver. His hands were small, the third finger of each hand crooked inward. His thumbs were thick. The skin would split at the top of his thumbnails from winter's cold and manual labor when home repair required his attention.

His skill did not transmit well to ponytails. He attempted this simple act one morning while Mom was in the hospital after the birth of my sister. His fingers kept fumbling, one grasp of thick hair slipping through his one hand while the other hand battled to retrieve my errant tresses. He finally succeeded in securing it, but I still clearly recall that I could not wait until Mom came home.

It was when Dad weaved palms that his hands turned elegant. Quick shuttles, those short fingers, charming the flat palm stalks into three-dimensional art. It was mesmerizing to watch those elongated fronds bloom into crosses, accordion-shaped, angle-perfect. He tried to teach me, daughter with hands exact in shape and form. All thumbs, my finished crosses crucified. Like his, my skin-split thumbs.

I'll try again, Dad, and arrange my work at your resting place. You and Mom will know I visited.

Palmistry

When dad weaved palms
   his hands spun elegant
   quick shuttles
   those short fingers

His hands were small
   third finger on each palm
   curved inward

His thumbs were thick
   fissure split
   from spite of winter
   moil of menial tasks.

Reluctant stalks
   charmed to art extraordinaire
   elongated fronds bloomed
     crosses
   accordion sculpted
   angle perfect
His Easter offering.

First mesmerized
   I tried to learn
   his method
   his daughter's hands
   exact in shape and form.

All thumbs, my finished
   crosses crucified
   like his, my skin-split thumbs
   no point returning to square
     one.

Bookends

———⊶⟨☙⟩⊷———

There's a set of bookends that could easily be older than I am. Two black metal (perhaps iron?) Scottish Terrier dogs, ears reared upwards toward what only they could hear—one each on a white marble base, 8" in height.

These canines held their domain on the night table in my parent's room. I discovered that my dad decided to move them downstairs to the top of the desk in the living room. I have always associated this pair with my father, who was always alert and tense—guarding what was precious. My imagination had me pretend they were bored upstairs and took a walk to seek a more exciting location. I made up stories about them. I believed they came alive at night while we slept, taking liberties with the couch, and licking my dolls' faces.

It never occurred to me to name these terriers. Perhaps I should.

Bye, Dad

⁃⦿⦿⦿⁃

My father insisted that he take me to school on my first day. He will not let my mother accompany us. Ah, Kindergarten—kids—playing with clay! Now I would find out where the older kids in the neighborhood go every day and what they do. Mom dresses me in a green plaid dress with narrow navy blue and red lines running in horizontal and vertical directions. My new black school shoes are so shiny; I don't want to wear them for fear that my walk could crease their appearance. Mom makes sure my long sausage hair strands stay in place. She secures them with bobby pins.

As we near the school building, something seems familiar. There's the church close by; there are the steps where Dad and I found the *Dick and Jane* book, the one we took home for my first reading lesson. A wonderful feeling comes over me.

As we climb the steps together, I wrestle my hand from dad's clenched fingers. I'm thinking, *I can't wait to get away from him and get into my classroom.* I run from him, run up the steps with kids I do not know, my long curls flying behind me. He calls my name. I don't look back.

Mom tells me years later that Dad didn't say a word to her when he came home. He sat down; no, mom said he *sank* down in a kitchen chair. When she asked him how it went, he gave her a forlorn look and said, *She pulled her hand away from me. She left me. She ran. She never looked back.*

The day came when my husband-to-be asked Dad for my hand in marriage. Later that evening, he sank down, yes, he *sank* in a kitchen chair and said to my mother, *I just came home from work, and now, she's getting married.* I've never looked back.

Twenty-Five Dollars and
The American Dream

⸻ ◦⟨⟨⟩⟩◦ ⸻

By extension of deeming my paternal grandparents as *Italian-Italian,* even though they were born here, I associated my father as *Italian-American,* as my mother was. He was born at home, which gave him the great pleasure of claiming that he didn't exist because no formal birth certificate was issued. But there was no doubt that he was alive, an authentic, ethnic Italian. He was as strong in his heritage as any ancestor before him. He grew up in one of the solid Italian pockets of South Philadelphia, across the street from the oldest Italian catholic church in the United States. Every sacred ritual was preserved and followed to the letter. Though very little Italian was spoken in the household, every nuance of culture thrived there, as it did throughout the area. One of the most solid connections was that of the singular fate of Mario Lanza living around the corner from their family. Lanza, considered the greatest living tenor of the twentieth century, the imprimatur that sealed his surroundings in the Italian way.

Similar to that cultural surrounding was the attitude that a husband was the decision-maker in the family. The acceptance that what the man of the house decided went unquestioned. If a strong personality was part of his mindset, there was no expectation of a willingness to comply with anyone's opinion.

One Sunday afternoon, we took a trip to a part of Philadelphia that wasn't familiar. I had no idea why we were standing outside a house that wasn't ours. Something in the air was happening; my ten-year-old mind was sure of it. Grandpop Arcidiacono kept stating, *Buy at the top of the hill! Don't wait!!* Another verbal exchange. Then, Grandpop put his hand in his pocket. I didn't see what happened next. I think mom was shooing me to the car. A few weeks later, movers placed our furniture inside that house that wasn't ours that day.

Many years later, mom told me what happened. My father's work commute lengthened. The plant where he worked relocated to a suburb of Philadelphia. The theory in those days was that if a family considered moving, it was best to do so before the children were teenagers, before their circle of friends and activities broadened. That Sunday, when dad took us on a drive, he had no idea what he might find. The banners waving new houses for sale were a chance encounter. When grandpop got out of the car, he took one look from where he stood—at the top of a high hill. He noticed that the houses further down the street were built to accommodate its slope. Where we stood, the houses were level. Grandpop knew what he had to do. He took my father aside and said this was the house to buy, the fourth one; the other three had already sold. Dad shook his head no. Grandpop came prepared. He surreptitiously gave my father what he needed.

Nearly fifty years passed. Our house never flooded. That day Grandpop Arci gave Dad the $25.00 deposit required to secure our next home. Dad was the champion listener that day. Grandpop was the champion survivor from living his former life at the mercy of Mount Etna.

Easter Parade

—◦◦◦—

Three women brought fourteen children into the world, and at no time was that more apparent than Easter.

In our neighborhood, Easter was a big deal, a big catholic deal. While we didn't have Easter egg hunts or egg rolling contests, our mothers' relentless need for us to dress to the nines bound us on Resurrection Day. They were at the helm on this one.

The three Italian-American women who played the most dramatic role in this regard were my mother and her two best friends in our Roxborough neighborhood. With all of us in tow, these three women not only dressed us but also prepared the Easter meal and our Easter baskets. They also dressed in a manner not employed during any other time of the year.

Mother of seven was a woman who was far too beautiful to be where she was but was there, nevertheless. She was tall, broad-shouldered, and blonde, with a profile worthy of the front page of Vogue magazine. She could wear a hat like no one else on the planet; the ones she chose were like her laugh—always easy to recognize from any distance. Her stature allowed her a regal air for the most dramatic earrings of any color, length, or shape, and they would complement her philosophy that she had, as she would say, *so little time to shine.* A stranger who knew nothing about her would never believe that this same woman would spend many hours and days making Easter ravioli to die for.

Mother of four, tall and beautiful as well, was dark-haired, blue-eyed, and magnificent at pizza making. A paradox in her own way, her *manos de oro* (hands of gold) could caress raw dough into the most divine-to-the-eye, most aromatic-to-the-olfactory-sense pie. The scent of the dough baking was enough to stop us in our tracks as we played outside. Her pizza crusts were as perfect as angels' wings, the only crusts I would want to eat. Her sense of style was not like mother of seven, but stylish, nevertheless.

Then there was my mother, the petite woman of three, who didn't have the height but had the Italian style sense of my grandmother. Mom completed the Fashion Triumvirate of the neighborhood. It eluded me whether they were trying to "one-up" the other women in the neighborhood or even each other. All I can say is that I always thought our mothers were the best-dressed, best-looking Italian women in Philadelphia.

Many years later, on a beautiful Saturday in May, our neighborhood had a reunion. By then, only my mother was alive. One of their children had also died the year before.

There were many cross-conversations as we enjoyed our time together. The topic of Easter came up. One of our mothers' sons immediately knew what I was getting at about our mothers. Up to that point, I had never voiced my opinion that I thought our mothers were the most beautiful in the neighborhood. To my surprise, he admonished me, *Linda, that's not nice!* He shot me a disapproving look, then added, with a sly grin, in his typical fashion, *True, but not nice!!!* Then he let out a laugh.

The time came to dress my daughter for her Easter parades. I scrutinized every detail. When the years of the resistant eyeroll came, the impatient weight shift from one Mary Jane shod foot to the other signaled her tween/teen years, I'd smile. I'd stand back, my arms folded, eyeing her from foot to hairline, cornering her until she met my fashion satisfaction. She'll call me now; *Mom, do you have a minute? I need you* to check her once more, from head to toe.

How little time we have to shine.

Cavete Carmen (Beware of Carmen)

———⟨∘⟨⊙⟩∘⟩———

I would never have imagined that the Olympia typewriter I received on my sixteenth birthday would provide a floodgate of opportunity for dad. He had a penchant for contacting businesses/companies when he believed a purchase did not live up to its claims. The *Consumer Reports* magazine found its way into our home, a bible source subscription for any product worth consideration. Thus armed, dad was a lion amidst the lambs of customer service.

My inaugural role as typist-in-residence became clear when dad decided the pen was mightier than a phone call. As a high school student on the academic track, I was unprepared for his stenographic commentary. Dad's handwriting was circular, fierce, tight, leaning to the right as if to storm the paper in the path of his fury, a hurricane with no eye. Deciphering small letters from capital ones was like separating the wheat from the chaff.

One summer afternoon, as dad surveyed our front yard, he glanced up at one of his bedroom windows. A recently purchased window-sized air conditioner hummed quietly two stories above him. The model number, clearly visible, caught his eye. Out of curiosity, he wrote the number down on his pocket-sized notepad.

I can still hear his yelling, *Linda, you have to type a letter for me!* Dad decided to check the purchase invoice. He hit the roof when the model number of our new air conditioner did not match the receipt.

In his Hell-hath-no-fury penmanship, he wrote a piercing complaint letter—a masterpiece of indignation which brought quick results. A fragment of a sentence comes to mind, *You thought your sleight of hand would pass unnoticed.* I also remember our loud disagreement over *sleight.* He took our well-beaten dictionary out of my offering hands, found the *sleight* word, and hummed a *Hmmm.* Sleight won out.

Dad received a phone call, an apology letter, a full refund (as I recall), and the air conditioner he originally selected. He considered this a triumph. I considered myself a candidate as a potential translator of the Rosetta Stone.

If Xerox had a Hall of Fame, dad's letters would be encased there. None of them were preserved in the copying light of day. (My Olympia typewriter still functions. *Ding!*)

Dad's Name Plate

———⚬❧⚬———

I hope someone threw dad's nameplate in the trash by accident. Perhaps, he had done it. Dad started hiding things in his waning years. No rhyme, no reason for his stashes or where he might have buried them. There was the time he hid coins in a secret drawer in the utility room closet. None of us knew about this hidden cubbyhole. I found it after his death when I noticed a color of paint that didn't quite match its surroundings.

It's an ordinary nameplate holder. It's one of those gold horizontal plastic ones, ridged at the top and the bottom so a nameplate could slide in. The walnut-colored faux wood nameplate with his name, Carmen A. Marrone, was lettered in white. This nameplate included an additional feature, a slightly used, yellow-colored No. 2 pencil taped across the top, black lettered, with the word *Unisys*.

Dad had taped the pencil to the top of the plate. I'm sure of it. The sharpened pencil, sharpened by him no doubt, at attention, streamlined. It's also possible that this was his last act as an employee when he retired from the company in 1984.

This pencil tells his life story. Computation. I remember how the figures spilled from his leaded instruments faster than the speed of thought. The maestro of numbers, reams of zeros and ones, worked from those years when his company was called *Univac*.

There was no doubt of his brilliance, overactive mind, and impatience. Whenever I sought his help with Math homework, his first response would always be, *"Get me a pencil and a piece of paper."* His explanations were far more thorough than my needs; often, he left me more confused than enlightened.

The man with the lead pencil helped to change the world. His contributions to the Univac I in 1951 and the Epcot Communication Center in Disneyworld in 1980 were unsung and undeniable. When I look at the nameplate, I hear people say his insight was so remarkable that only a few could understand him.

His numbers and my words locked horns through our lifetime, bound inexorably by lead.

Memorial Days

⎯⎯ ∾ᘒᘒᗘ∾ ⎯⎯

December 7, 2018

Seventy-seven years ago today, December 7, 2018, the U.S. faced its first September 11th. On that beautiful Sunday morning, the paradise sky of Pearl Harbor was rent asunder by the two infamous attacks that changed that day to the "day that will live in infamy." That day, a new shoot sprouted from the seeds planted by the Great Immigration Wave and bore fruit during The Great Depression. This fruit ultimately blossomed into The Greatest Generation.

Those of us of that particular age didn't realize that when our fathers went to work every day and provided for us, they carried within them the memories of that fateful day. They fought the war, came home, put it behind them, and the rest continued to be history.

∾ᘒᗘᘒ∾

One evening, as my father and I watched TV, a newsreel appeared, one of those "moments of history" snippets. There, in black and white, was a ship with an overspill of young men elbowing their way to the camera's view. So many that it seemed the ship might sink from top-heaviness. Cheering, waving, and yelling, "Hi, Mom!" crowded the air. They waved frantically, smiling, jostling one another in an eagerness to cross the sea to save the world. It was wartime. Joyous faces on the road to victory. George M. Cohan's "Over There" in the background soundtrack, the determined favorite stanza blaring that they won't return until the war ended:

"We'll be over/ We're coming over/ And we won't come back til its over/ Over there."

It seemed the fervor of their youthful conviction, the whoop of these seafaring soldiers, could have been enough to sink this ship.

It occurred to me that those young men were as old as I was. I asked my father if it ever crossed his mind that he would not return from the War. He reared his head back ever-so-slightly, paused, looked me square in the eye, and said, *You know, I never gave it a thought that I wouldn't return.* Even he seemed surprised at his reaction.

⋰⋰⊙⋱⋱

It hit me very hard when I visited Pearl Harbor in 1977. The printed rules of comportment were in my hand and on signage at the boarding dock. The pamphlet and the entrance sign went something like this:

> The USS Arizona is **not** a to be mistaken for a tourist attraction. Every level of respectful behavior is expected and required. Swimsuits are not appropriate. This is a cemetery, not a sight-seeing tour. Photos are acceptable, provided they reflect the somber memory of the Memorial.

We learned the bomb's impact was so forceful that many of the crew were trapped and entombed in this vessel they served—an active gravesite of eleven hundred and seventy-seven souls.

The assembly hall crosses over the ship. Seven large windows span each wall and ceiling to signify the date's permanency, the twenty-one windows an eternal twenty-one-gun salute. I stepped in and saw a large hole cut into one area of the memorial floor, a direct view of the submerged wreckage below, the USS Arizona a few feet below me. Flowers floated there, dropped by visitors. The realization that I was standing over a breathing grave overcame me. Then, I heard a sound that brought on nausea. That "golumb" sound. *Gol-umb.* The "golumb" sound of oil splotches that still rose to the water's surface from the bombing, *Gol-umb*, over and over, a slow volley of the sound of the dead. An eerie pulse, recoiling and mesmerizing. I could not steady myself, could not smell or feel anything—the sense of *Gol-umb.*

Gol-umb ~ splotches of oil
surface   hollow sound—
amoeba contours

Gol-umb ~ a spread veil
heaves   yaws   heartbeats
of what could have been.

A crushing experience. A sound I still hear but have never heard again. I told myself this was The Pearl of our country. The Pearl is not in anyone's way. Servicemen and servicewomen stationed there believed they had died and went to Heaven.

And on December 7, 1941, eleven hundred and seventy-seven did.

And now I know why I remain unnerved, what sets this apart from any other cemetery. I stood above a once-bustling ship that hardly had a moment to greet that morning. And now the Golumb knells, from that day to eternity.

⁓⊙⊙⊙⁓

Today, I think of those waving young men. For many, theirs was a one-way wave. Today, I think of my father, our fathers, who went about their lives and rarely spoke of their experiences during those years. Today, I think of the men I've met throughout my career, the fathers of my friends and family, who were courageous, heroic, and silent, their deeds kept deep within them, surfacing after their death many years later.

⁓⊙⊙⊙⁓

We never imagined we would live through our own Pearl Harbor sixty years later, on that beautiful Tuesday morning of September 11, 2001, when two infamous attacks in New York, one at the Pentagon in

Washington, D.C., and one diverted plane crash in Shanksville, Pennsylvania would bring another "day that will live in infamy." Many of our fathers who fought in the war were still alive that day. I wonder if their memory of Pearl Harbor emerged.

May they all Rest in Peace.

The Underground Life of Jesus Christ, Superstar

⟡

Every Easter, I think of the underground life of *Jesus Christ, Superstar.* *That foul piece of supposed music will have no place in this house!* my father roared.

The *Superstar* concept album debuted in 1970, and in our neck of the woods, the heavily Catholic Northwest section of Philadelphia, it was nothing short of heresy. Being heavily Catholic meant Mass every Sunday with your family. Being heavily Catholic meant you went to confession at least once a month. Being heavily Catholic meant you graduated from your solidly catholic grade school, then graduated from your local solidly catholic high school. Some of us continued our solidly catholic education when we graduated from a solidly catholic college. What else could one do but return to your solidly catholic church to be married?

My father became livid as he observed the priests from the pulpit, the articles in the *Catholic Standard and Times* newspaper, and the nuns at my high school alma mater in holy fits over this blasphemous telling of the final days of Jesus.

Dad was appalled at what he heard, this ceaseless, gossipy pontification. We knew he had not listened to a single note of this libretto. We knew better than to protest over his fire and brimstone rant.

So, my siblings and I did the next best thing. We went underground with it.

∽◦◦◦∽

Luckily (or perhaps it was the shrewdness of the producers), the album was a darkish brown color, which lent itself, no pun intended, to an infinite number of hiding places. One day, Dad came home from work earlier than expected; Mom was having a conniption as the album was in full view on the kitchen counter. We learned early in life not to make any sudden movements when we were doing something degenerative when he was around, to not call attention to ourselves. We calmly passed the album through the faux window into the dining room as dad entered the kitchen, our contraband out of sight. We reversed our tactic when he re-entered the dining room.

Remember that this behavior was not unique to our neighborhood alone; we lived in a heavily Catholic area. We became self-groomed Masters of Subterfuge.

∽◦◦◦∽

Fast forward to many years later, when our local Public TV station aired a production of *Superstar*. My Dad got wind of it and decided to view the program. Two seconds after it was over, he called me. I was white-knuckled as I picked up the phone, fully expecting to hear for the zillionth time that we should be excommunicated for having anything to do with/taking any enjoyment from the performance.

But that's not what happened. Dad expressed total amazement, stating how great the music was and that now, he "got the message." When I was too flabbergasted to respond, he thought I had fainted.

Linda, are you still there? When my heart restarted, I answered, *Yes, Dad, I'm here.*

He wanted to know about Andrew Lloyd Webber and Tim Rice, the duo behind this rock opera. He remarked: *That one song, "I Don't Know How to Love Him." That's beautiful. I don't remember ever hearing it before.*

Sensing his awestruck mood, I interjected, *It makes Mary Magdalen and Jesus human beings, doesn't it?*

After a moment of silence, he answered, *Yes, it does.*

Then, he sighed, the closest behavior I would get to an apology. I reminded him of what he told me long ago: good music is good music, no matter when it's written or the motivation behind it.

I knew what would come next because Dad was Dad.

He asked, *Okay, where did you kids hide the album?*

Silent tears of laughter rolled down my face as I twisted the phone cord.

You're not gonna tell me, are you?

Nope! I answered, *And it's too late at night for you to come after me!*

He exploded with laughter. Jesus most assuredly rose from the dead again after hearing this exchange.

What is most compelling about *Superstar* was how my thoughts about Holy Week and Jesus and His followers changed significantly. While the production squarely places Judas on a blasphemous pedestal from the viewpoint of the Church's teachings, it shifts the focus to the humanity of Jesus and the people around him. Some songs are so strong in their struggles; the phrasing is outstanding. The most potent line in all of Rock Music for me is the line that Jesus sings in the Garden of Gethsemane, "Then, I was inspired, now I'm sad and tired." There have been times in my life when I have genuinely felt that way. During our Catholic formative years, there was minimal emphasis or explanation about this aspect of Jesus and his disciples. This portrayal transformed me as no other music did.

What upset us more than anything else was that our parents accepted words of authority on blind faith and did not take the time to listen to the music for their sake or ours. They missed the point entirely by not taking the time to give us a chance. As we saw it, there's a little bit of Jesus, Judas, Mary, and Pilate in all of us; they will always be in all of us until we leave this earth.

The last movement of *Superstar*, *John's Psalm*, is very brief, subdued, and without singing. I have played this piece many, many times. For all its soothing, diametrically opposed sound, it conjures a permanent image for me of what immediately happened after Jesus died. My mind sees Him being removed from the cross, placed in His Mother's arms, then placed in the tomb without the fanfare and the adoring crowds. I think of Mary, Jesus' Mother, who started on her journey alone, pregnant at fifteen, then with Joseph, losing Joseph (who died before Jesus did), losing Jesus, and coming full circle, alone once more.

I cannot imagine more piercing heartbreak.

The Election that Changed the World

———⁓◦❦◦⁓———

November 5, 2008

Contrary to what you might expect to read, in my opinion, the election of Barack Obama was not the election that changed the world. That event occurred in 1952 when a group of ten men assembled in a building to tabulate the results of the Eisenhower election.

That building, located in the Spring Garden Section of Philadelphia, at Ridge Ave and Callowhill Streets, is a modest two-story facility, one that is typical of most business structures of that period. Six Univac computers were located on the test floor. The company at the time was called Remington Rand Inc., founded by J. Presper Eckert and John Mauchly, graduates of the University of Pennsylvania.

One of those ten technicians was my father.

That night, he and the other technicians set out to do something unprecedented—they would predict the Eisenhower versus Stevenson election results.

News commentators Charles Collingwood and Walter Cronkite, both stationed in New York, covered the event. It worked out according to plan. The technicians determined early that evening that Eisenhower won the election.

There was great reluctance on the news anchors' part to make this announcement. The newscasters, and probably CBS, simply did not trust this new-fangled gadget. The technicians were bursting. Eckert and Mauchly, to quote my father, were *pissed*. Their reluctance was understandable, considering the prior election of 1948 and the infamous "Dewey Wins" headline that caused the Chicago Daily Tribune major embarrassment. Eventually, the news outlets did start reporting the group's prediction.

Five months after Eisenhower was elected, I was born.

I spoke to my Dad about that election on November 5, 2008. He reminisced that he couldn't believe that was fifty-six years ago and how times have changed. He thanked me and wanted to know why I would bring this up during every election. I would always tell him it was because he was one of the first men in the world to know something monumental before the rest of the world knew it, communicated to the world by a "new-fangled gadget."

That 2008 election would be the last he would experience. Dad died on January 21, 2010. This November 3rd, I will hear him say once more, *That was really something!*

Matadaughter

I parted this page with words
     the bull grunted in my father's mind.

The first time dad changed
came from nowhere
my question made him
    stop and say
I can't remember

He combed his hair with
    frantic fingers
a rush of no recall
  his blue eyes   searched
asked air for rescue

                Red bull eyes   appeared
                 locked with mine.
               Who are you?   Eyes
                   bloodied fury
                horned eyebrows
                   breath snorting
                     I   screamed

Dad's eyes flashed blue   again
          breath quiet
What just happened?

                              Again, bull eyes
                         dreaded red returned
                    My level gaze   fearless
                         flared interrogating
                         How dare you take
                            my father's mind?
                         I have no fear of you!

          Our eyes   tangoed for my father
     in charged circles   paced   scraping ground

I moved in closer
My voice took over—
          Dad, it's macaroni night
          your favorite gravy too!
          Let's talk at dinner
          of binary code, of decimals,
          of ENIAC and Univac.
The red receded   blue
          Dad smiled   we spoke
of routine things   surrounding him
          with a cape of all I knew
of him and I.

Reparation for Omission

For all their differences, my parents were a pair par excellence on the dance floor. Theirs was the Swing Era, the era before couples began to dance more or less independently of one another. Their sixty years of dance moves, from ingenue couple to "Old Smoothies," evoked many an "ooh" and "ah" on those occasions when they permitted themselves to shine.

As my father grew older, he attempted a joke that he wanted us to bury him in his black dress shoes. He hoped he would predecease my mother and be ready to take her upon his arm on her arrival in Heaven, prepared to dance with her for eternity in those very shoes.

Half of his wish came true. In the unexpected crisis that took him from us in 2010, his black dress shoes did not join him in his casket. Our discovery was discovered too late. When a violent downpour descended on us on the day of his funeral ceremony, we felt every drop of his watery reprimand.

Six years later, redress, best expressed by my heartfelt poem, in their honor.

Swing Your Departed

My father's horizontal pose is shoeless,
Discovery too late to rectify,
We hide our shoeless gaffe with blanket blue.

Torrential rain from Hell, his parting shot,
Water engulfs and muds us at the cemetery plot.
When Mom joins Dad, we have our second chance,

We hide our shoeless gaffe with blanket blue,
Mom's feet so small no one would know our "shoe-in."
Now, both departed, joined forever souls.

Shoe satisfied, there is that final signal,
My parents dance in Heaven on this day,
A whirlwind blast descends itself on Ardmore.

A blast beyond the norm,
We know that they are dancing up a storm.

Celebrating the Life of My Mother

———— ✺ ————

July 18, 2016

Today, we have come together to celebrate the life of Mary Arcidiacono Marrone, a daughter, a sibling, a spouse, an aunt, a mother, a
mother-in-law, a grandmother, a neighbor, a friend, and a second mother
to several of our friends. Mom's life from the very beginning was one of
sharing. Mom entered the world as Maria, with Uncle Vince as her fra-
ternal twin. Her parents named her for a sister she had never met, a child
who died in 1920 after a brief illness. Upon Mom's arrival, Grandpop
exclaimed with joy, "This is my Little Dol-lee!!" Indeed, Mom was a
petite, beautiful child, affectionately named "Little Mary" to distinguish
her from her taller cousin, "Big Mary," with the same name.

Mom's parents, Gaetano and Sebastiana, came from Sicily in 1910
and 1912, part of the great Italian immigration influx settling in South
Philadelphia. As a first-generation Italian, Mom grew up in a loving
home with three brothers but never had the opportunity to know her
grandparents. It was a fairly common occurrence for this generation.
Many grandparents decided to remain in their birthplace. Mom vowed
that her children would not be bereft of such a gift. We are forever grateful and indebted to her for this resolve.

Mom was part of the "Greatest Generation." She was surrounded
by family and an ethnic neighborhood that struggled with the Great

Depression and World War II. Shortly after the War, she went on a trip to the Pocono Mountains and met two young ladies who would eventually introduce her to our father, Carmen. They married in 1951 and spent over sixty years together. Ironically, on the day of her passing, Mom was back in the Poconos.

Mom was greatly loved, and I can say that without reservation. She not only gave us the blessings of grandparents, but she also brought me the blessings of two siblings. I clearly remember both occasions of their arrival home. As she often said, her ambition was to raise *three different people,* and she achieved that goal as there was no lack of opinion under our roof.

Her social wires were natural and sweet; she was kind, generous, and humble. She moved comfortably among us Baby Boomers. When we moved to Roxborough, she mothered all of us "Outback Kids," as we called ourselves, with all the other mothers. Mom was an excellent cook and made the world's best Italian Wedding Chicken Soup and cannoli, shells included, by hand (dangerous in those days). She baked amazing cheese pies. Mom loved to feed our friends, which they greatly appreciated and still comment about with a sense of awe and gratitude. Mom was a natural beauty, petite and fastidious beyond reason. Her last act on this earth was fixing her hair, which was a source of great pride all her life, a forgivable vanity.

Once we were educated and grown, Mom endeavored to return to the working world. But Mom was called to the caretaking of our three grandparents during their later years and our Dad, as his mental state deteriorated until his demise.

Mom dearly loved little children and was finally blessed in 1993 when our daughter arrived, followed by our nephew one week later and his brother four years later. A happier grandmother never existed.

So, thanks Mom, for all you did for us, for teaching us that good neighbors are a gift from God, and for praying the rosary every day. And thank you, Roe, my sister, and my heroine, for your exquisite, loving care of our beloved Mother.

Your loving daughter,
Linda Marrone Romanowski

What is a Father?

January 24, 2010

A father is a person who loves his spouse, who brings home siblings to share a lifetime, who provides for his family, who rescues baby birds that fall from nests, who teaches you to ride a bicycle (keep pedaling!), who admonishes you not to lie to him ever, who commands you to *do the right thing* always, who cares for both sets of parents, who loves our cousins and our spouses, who adores his grandchildren, who served our country.

Our father possessed all these attributes and so much more. He was strong; he was brilliant. There wasn't anything he couldn't fix. He was excellent in emergencies. He grew the best zoysia grass in Philadelphia.

We were always proud that he was a contributor to the success of Univac I, the world's first commercial computer.

I think of his outstanding pancakes and being known as "Crazy Uncle Carmen." When we moved to Roxborough, I was ten years old. Our new environment was so different from our former home in South Philadelphia, and with a new car, my young mind thought we were wealthy. After we moved, I wrote letters frequently to my best friend from my former neighborhood, and I attribute what writing skills I possess to that activity.

He had an unerring ear for classical music, and the recordings that changed our living room into a concert hall will be with me always. His determination that his children had a college education, *that piece of paper,* and his unfailing devotion to our grandparents made our lives complete as nothing else could.

And so, for all I've said, I say my eternal "Thank You" once more, thanks for helping to change the world, thanks for helping to save that baby bird. Thanks for caring for our grandparents, for loving them all as your parents. And thank you for granting us our American Dream.

With love, your ever-grateful daughter,
Linda Marrone Romanowski

Section III

AMERICAN – ITALIAN

Ravioli Revenge

———⌘———

We grew up in a world that did not measure time in a calendar-centric way. The Italian approach was and remains food centric. We knew when it was summer (watermelon), we knew when it was fall (winemaking), we knew when it was Christmas (pizzelles), and at Easter, springtime, it was ravioli.

Grandmom Marrone commanded the ravioli-making enterprise at the house she and her daughter and son-in-law shared. No space was left unclaimed in their tiny kitchen to prepare, cook, and serve the world's best Easter entrée. My aunts and my mother, aproned and attentive, waited for Grandmom to hold court. The men and the children kept their distance under the watchful TV eye of CBS in the living room.

I was bored sitting on the couch. I was soon to be three years old, and in 1956, Easter fell on my birthday, April 1st, a rare occurrence. I resorted to crawling into grandpop's lap. I could see some of the bustling in that forbidden room, the massive pot of boiling water hissing in time to background Italian music. My aunts scurried to and fro, placing the delicate ravioli into the steamy cauldron. Mom stood by the doorway. I jumped down from grandpop's legs and ran to her. I pulled at her apron; she knew what I wanted. That's why she positioned herself at the cookery threshold.

No! she mouthed to me. She rolled her eyes toward the living room, where I knew I should be. Undaunted, I approached my grandmother.

I asked to help. *Linda, get out of my kitchen!* She bellowed, shaking her wooden spoon at me. When I refused to move, she stomped her foot at me. Mom intervened, steering me back to grandpop's chair.

As I looked back, I glanced upward. There were rows and rows of handmade ravioli on the dining room table. Hundreds of satiny pillows crimped closed by tines of the forks, pressed into the dough by hand. They were raw and slightly floury, awaiting their transfer from table to pot. As soon as I could, I slipped away from grandpop's sleepy posture and ventured back toward my mother. I peered into the kitchen on tip-toe. I sulked. Grandmom would not allow me to join them.

I fully recall the moment I became incensed. Those ravioli tempted me from their place high on the table. When I noticed the end of the tablecloth draped within my reach, my mind locked me to action. *Oh, yeah?!* I thought. I grabbed the dangled end of the tablecloth and yanked it with all my three-year-old might.

There was a dull *whomp* sound. Scores of ravioli hit the breakfront at the end of the table. Some of them hit full force, hanging like hinges, sticking to the glass-paned sections of the furniture. Floury warriors, clinging to certain death, resting place unknown. Dozens more hit the server on the opposite side. Some fell to the floor. Then, the descent of Grandmom, her stealth bomber hearing, detecting my maneuver. When she screamed, I clutched at the tablecloth again; more ravioli flew in several directions. Grandmom was a breath away from striking me when I felt pulled high into the air. Grandpop swung me away from her. My soft-spoken Savior raised his voice to her, *Rose, this is your fault. I heard everything. All you needed to do was to give her a ball of dough.*

That ended it. I planted my face in grandpop's neck for the rest of the day. I felt his kind, smooth-shaven face against my cheek. My three-year-old nose categorized his balm-scented cologne in my psyche forever.

⌒◯◯⌒

I have no recollection of hearing his voice again. Shortly after that 1956 Easter, grandpop was diagnosed with throat cancer. Doctors re-moved his larynx; he spoke no longer. My child's mind reasoned that his silence, handsome blue eyes, and stately build must surely prove that he was God. He died in 1957 at the age of fifty-nine. My grandmother out-lived him by forty-one years. My father never got over his early loss. The kind words Grandmom Marrone always spoke about my grandfather, how greatly my mother and the family loved him, hold him cherished in my memory. I was granted the privilege as his first-born grandchild, the only one with any direct memory connection to him.

Faith in Smoke

———⌑⌒⌑———

G randpop Arci's lack of church attendance set me at odds with
the guilt the nuns inflicted on every first-grade, pre-First Com-
municant. The religious sisters threatened that we would go to Hell under no uncertain terms if we did not attend weekly Mass.

The thought that grandpop would become as charred as the ashes of
his cigars in the afterlife, in the relentless fires of Eternal Damnation, terrified me. I tried to explain this nun-driven horror to my mother. I told
her grandpop told me he did not like going to church because he couldn't
smoke during the service.

Mom attempted to comfort me by pointing out that Grandmom
Arci spent enough time in church to make up for him and her. Mom
told me not to listen to the nuns. Ignoring them was my first defiant act
toward religious authority.

FAITH AND SONG

Grandmom Arci possessed the most beautiful voice. Her soprano
notes hit the High C vocal range without effort.

When Grandmom sang in church, no one need turn their head to see
who was singing. Everyone knew it was Sebastiana. Anna (her nickname)
kept to herself, worrying each rosary bead with her tireless fingers, prayer,
and song—her sacred litany.

The old radio in her kitchen was her orchestra that accompanied her operatic escape from her world. No word of English ever announced its presence during those afternoons. As she sang from her Sicilian soul, was she a young girl again? Did grandmom's voice reach her homeland?

Connections

Grandmom   stitching
my writing
each paired
to an act
of repetition.
Threads   words
threads of words
words in   threads.

Grandpop   weaving
grapes pressing
my words   pressed out
words   weave
words press
each paired
to an act
of repetition.

I   their thread
their warp
their woof
shuttled within them
stitched in the present
stitched by their past
sewn to their legacy.
I   basting shuttled wings.

Mary Janes

———⟡⟡⟡———

White Cap shoe polish was the crème de la crème polish for white Mary Jane shoes when I was growing up. Blue box, with the face of a blonde-haired, blue-eyed white child set in a black background, this portrait encircled by a white band. Now it appears under the name of Hollywood Sani-White with a yellow label reading "non-toxic" under the face of the original child.

Shoe polishing was an art form back then, a source of pride, a show of class. Shoe polishing required a drying strategy. Polished shoes needed a separate place to "set," airy but not windy, a spot not too hot or too cold. Drying time was a consideration but testing a hidden area of the shoe for doneness was imperative. Miscalculated dryness meant a specific white-shoe-polish-set-for-life stain on whatever the shoe might touch. Permanent. Final.

It was a Spring morning when my mother set my first pair of white Mary Janes on the lid of the metal trash can. The cover was wide, the trash can the desired height, and the early hour sunny, calm, and quiet. Mom usually left my shoes to dry on the kitchen windowsill, but it was such a lovely day, too beautiful to leave them "set" indoors. Outdoor air eased the detection of the scent of dryness, an essence faintly related to white-painted fences.

At that time, mom readied the three of us, aged five and under, to visit my aunt. One child in the coach, two holding the coach's handle on either side, we walked to her house, returning home later in the afternoon.

By that time, my Mary Janes would be dry. Mom settled us and went into the backyard to retrieve them. The trash can was there; the lid was there; the shoes were gone. Startled, mom did a mental check of her morning routine. She retraced her steps; for sure, she had not left my shoes on the windowsill. Mom went outside again; perhaps my shoes had fallen in the garden patch.

Mom heard the distant rumble of the sanitation truck. She reasoned that one of the sanitation workers might have taken the shoes, assuming she had discarded them because of their location on the trash can lid. Someone in the neighborhood saw mom in the yard and asked what was wrong. Mom explained what she thought might have happened. A day or so later, she found out the missing shoes were the talk of the neighborhood. This wildfire had everything to do with the fact that some of the sanitation workers were African American. Unsavory epithets came from the lips of the least expected.

Mom was horrified. Her surmise was a musing comment to a neighbor, not a fact, not explained as one. Hers was an innocent remark, followed by self-deprecation for her foolish act. She explained and re-explained herself to anyone willing to listen. I believe Mom contacted the sanitation department to report there was no wrongdoing. Anyone walking down the alley that day could have taken those Mary Janes. Anyone.

As young as I was, I knew something was amiss. Mom's distracting behavior was a signal that something serious had occurred. It sounded as if a neighborhood adult dropped the "N-word" in my hearing range. Mom sprang into action. There must have been a sharp verbal exchange between her and the offensive speaker. She pulled me into the house and slammed the door shut.

She sat me down and told me about my shoes. After returning from my aunt's house, she told me they were not where she had left them. She explained what she thought might have happened. Mom told me not to worry; she would replace my missing pair.

Then she told me what really worried her. Worry that neighbors might say terrible things about good men that I might overhear. Worry that neighbors might start an argument with innocent men who did nothing wrong. Worry that her children might hear terrible words aimed at these good men, ugly, false, damaging names. I learned that the few people I saw during my five years of life whose skin was darker than mine had not spent more time in the sun than everyone else.

My emotions still run high beneath my surface when I recall mom's courage in attempting to correct a perceived wrong, a wrong that others so quickly and willingly believed. Mom placed herself at risk of the loss of friendship. She hid her feelings when some neighbors consequently shunned her. She gave up their comradery and instilled in me the realization that I was brought up in a household devoid of overt prejudice—no racial or ethnic slurs reverberated through our house, no curse words, not even ones that could be disguised in Italian speech. That day when mom sat me down and set me straight, she put me straight forever. I was to view each person as they presented themselves to me. I was to give each person a chance always. All the other things she said to me that day condensed themselves to these few words.

The very last thing I remember her saying was that she believed my Mary Janes made a little girl happy. Maybe they were her first Mary Janes. Maybe her happiness made her parents happy. That would be enough to make me happy. That was more than enough for me for one day.

Illusion of Choice

———∽✧∾———

I couldn't have been much older than seven when it came to light that I was knock-kneed. I recall that one leg was shorter than the other—my right leg. Doctors told my parents that I also had scoliosis, not a severe case, but enough to create an impediment to my knees aligning. This condition is not uncommon in youngsters. Nature's growth course tends to straighten out most children's bodies by age five. For children in my age group, the traditional remedy was corrective shoes.

Corrective shoes. Words of dread. Words synonymous with Sherman Tanks. The corrective shoe logic reasons that constant foot support would gradually entice the legs and the knees to function in tandem. There is no one "cure timetable." The proof of this prevailing wisdom of the 1950s and 1960s is scant to non-existent. The one-track words of advice are to wear these corrective shoes every day, every waking hour. The silver lining is that, unlike dental braces that imprison errant teeth, one's feet are free from bath time to bedtime to the following day. Wiggling my toes during those paradise hours of feet freedom never felt so good.

After my diagnosis, my first shoe-shopping visit starts as an ordinary walk with my mother to a long-gone store whose name eludes me. I can summon a memory of a long, narrow place with burgundy-colored upholstered chairs. The smell of leather predominates, a rich, thick, somewhat smoky shoe scent in the air. Now and then, a peek of a glimpse of poie de soie slippers. From their soft silky fabrics, a pleasant undefined fragrance.

Mom directs me to the children's section, where the Kingdom of Buster Brown shoes presides. Mom speaks with a salesman while I position myself in a chair directly in front of two pairs of shoes, my size, by some odd chance. There they are, the indestructible dark burgundy-brown corrective Sherman Tanks. Next to this pair are the most beautiful pair of moccasins. Fawn colored, soft to the eye, leathery smooth, velvety to the touch, with a faint scent-of-wood-in-a-breeze. Perfectly tied tassels of the same color are attached to the upper front of each shoe, with exquisite beading of a wildflower below each tie—tiny beads of reds and blues, a pin-dot of white here and there.

These moccasins are on my feet before mom finishes her discussion with the shoe clerk. She half-notices my ethereal Pocahontas Walk of the Divine. I am in a forest with the legendary little girl, this favored daughter of Chief Powhatan called "playful one," beside me.

The Sherman Tanks come next. These clunkers aren't called Sherman Tanks without good reason. The salesman laces them up; my feet become corseted. I can scarcely move in these instruments of torture. Mom reads my mind and says these shoes are supposed to feel that way. In time, I will break them in. I know what's coming next.

Mom asks me which pair of shoes I want. Two pairs of shoes right before my eyes, calling my name for two different reasons. My feet are like lead, my heart just as heavy, and my tongue sticks to the roof of my mouth. My hands sweat. I swallow hard; I sit down, look down at the floor, and choose the corrective shoes.

Out of the corner of my eye, I see mom breathe a sigh of relief. She knows mine was an empty, cornered decision, a chosen lie. She doesn't protest when I do not leave the store with my choice on my feet to soften her conscience. As we leave the store, I won't look back at the fawn-colored beauties left behind. Other little girls crowd around them now, gazing at them, entranced, one of them destined to walk in my Pocahontas treasures.

My mother and I know what we have done to one another. Mom, with her shoe fetish, wanted me to feel I had a choice. I, wanting so much to have a choice, knew I had no option but to choose what I didn't want.

Wrongdoing

———⟋⟍———

Dad's intellect was such that he could not always understand why people didn't "get it" when he understood things so quickly. It seems to be a common flaw in those gifted with superior intellect. Perhaps this was a factor in his pervasive anxiety that he refused to recognize. He unknowingly got in his own way, a self-ignorance that surely canonized my mother to sainthood.

You're doing it wrong—Dad's mantra. So often, when I'd try to do what he told me, what I did wouldn't please him. I'd break out in a sweat (I'd ask myself, *What did he say?*). Many times, that phrase knee-jerking its way into my brain without forethought. Once when I was nine years old and struggling with a math problem, he boomed the correct answer again and again. I broke out in red blotches. Big, red blotches. Down the center back of my neck, blotches.

These blossoming blotches spread like wings across my shoulders and down my arms. The skin on my stomach resembled measles. Wherever parts of my skin met were the worst areas. Underarms were a blotching nightmare. Meanwhile, up from my neck, red blotch bumps appeared behind my ears. My forehead fevered in blotches. My hands shook. I could feel a creepiness down my legs.

I was a breathing hive. Was there a blotchy rash in my throat? I dared not touch my tongue. Tears slid down my face, rivulets of pain as my salty pleas hit my cheeks. I was hyperventilating, feeling close to anaphylactic shock, another reaction to the antigen of his voice.

Mom came into the room, and I waved her away. I did not want her to calm me; no, that wasn't it. I didn't want her to do anything to set him off again. My ears hit their limit of the *You're doing it wrong* litany. I stopped crying, slid my books closed, and mumbled goodnight, no less reddened, no more enlightened. I stole my way up the stairs. All I wanted was to die between cool bedsheets and darkness. Maybe that was something I could do correctly.

Framed Words

———⌇⊶⊷⌇———

Ihave a framed quote on my dining room server, a revived memory of the omnipresent ashtray in Grandmom Arci's living room. Its original setting was a flat cream-colored ceramic dish with slightly scalloped edges outlined in earth brown, the size of the palm of my eight-year-old hand. It was a self-contained platitude, the words in a portrait layout.

When I was old enough to realize the writing on the ashtray was not English, I asked my Grandfather what it said. He read:

Acqua te fa bene, ma vino fa cantare l'uomone.

His hazel eyes twinkled; he tucked his cigar that often rested on those words in his shirt pocket.

Leenda, he chuckled. *It says, "Water is good-a for you, but wine makes-a men sing."* I traced over this motto he lived by with hesitant fingers, repeating his words. Some ashes buried themselves in the corners of the plate, their yellow stain of trapped ashes stuck under my nails. Yellow stains under my nails were the telltale giveaway. Hiding my hands behind my back would never protect me from Grandmom's nostrils. She would know, and he would know she would know. Drama was nothing new in their constant tango over cigar smoking in the house.

At the time, Grandpop's translation of the Italian proverb didn't clarify the meaning to me any more than his speaking it in Italian. *Someday,* I thought to myself, *this will make sense.*

Years of annual family winemaking eventually brought those words into aromatic focus. My coming of vintage moment arrived years after a grape pressing when I placed the ashtray in Grandpop's hands after he corked the last cask. Our eyes and smiles locked in recognition as family members drank and sang "Oh, Solo Mio" and other opera fragments.

More years passed, and when the ashtray disappeared, I was beyond consoling. No one in the family could attest to its whereabouts. We doubted that it had broken. Somehow, it went missing in the final stages of Grandpop's relocation to our house.

One Christmas, an Italian-born coworker, presented me with the Italian translation of this sacred motto, those prodigal words so bittersweet to my soul. I preserved this precious document in a golden frame in memory of the gold paper bands wedded around those cherry-earthy fragrant house transgressors that so vexed my grandmother. All those years of wondering, searching in vain for this Italian proverb that came to a dead end, were saved in the end when he presented those words to me.

I want that ashtray found. We are still resurrecting surprising treasures in the boxes Mom left behind in her passing. I pray for that long-sought-after find as we continue to divide and conquer my parents' possessions.

La ricerca ti fa bene, ma trovare mi fara cantare. Searching is good for you but finding it will make me sing.

Christian Street Caruso

—◦◦◦◦—

My quest to visit the Mario Lanza Museum would not be thwarted. Its most recent South Philadelphia location, 7th, and Montrose Streets, was sold to a developer. The opening of the new site at 12th and Reed Streets is scheduled for late spring 2019.

I contacted my cousin, who lives across the street from the now "former" museum, to inform her of my informal pilgrimage plan. She would join my husband Ken and me on our visit to the church. Our trip would include visiting the Mario Lanza mural, Lanza's birthplace, the Italian Market, and St. Mary Magdalen de Pazzi Church.

A venture by foot and by car awaited us. We were grateful that this day was Ash Wednesday, March 6, 2019, the first day of Lent in the Roman Catholic Church. That meant the church would be open for the Lenten Service. Perfect timing.

My husband and I chose to visit the mural first for parking, traffic, and optimal light. Diane Keller painted it in 1997 with the approval of the Mario Lanza Institute. Its design is a very well-done timeline. It is one hundred feet long, and the height shifts to four stories as its canvas is a townhouse condominium. The working surface played well to Lanza, larger than life with a voice to emphasize it. People said that when Mario Lanza sang, you could hear him a block away.

The mural's focal point depicts Lanza in his early prime, clutching his temples as he sings the Othello Monologue from the 1956 movie

Serenade, a role that was enough to make him immortal. Moving to the right is a Victrola turntable, Pagliacci, the clown in an oval frame. At the apex, the off-centered centerpiece, Lanza is the greatest tenor of all time in *The Great Caruso,* his most famous film (1951).

Local talk has it that Keller placed a boom box on her scaffold as she painted the mural and reawakened South Philadelphia to the resonating, profound notes of her subject. The August to October days were as much an inspiration to her as those who gathered to reminisce and enlighten those unaware of this Titan of Tenors. Lanza's face might have been four stories above my own, yet his gaze met mine. And that brought me back to a prior era of a long-buried memory.

Both sets of grandparents lived within a mile of each other in South Philadelphia. The Lanza family lived on Christian Street, near my father's house on Montrose Street; this area is known as Bella Vista. Lanza was an only child, four years older than my father. Our families did not know one another personally.

My mother's house was on tiny, one-way Fernon Street. It was situated in the area now named Southwark Eastern Neighborhood Enterprises, far too gentrified a term for such a modest environment. I recall hearing it called "Southwark" when my grandparents were alive. A far more memorable comment regarding location came from mom, who often remarked that the part in my hair looked like Passyunk Avenue, an angled street that seemed to appear and disappear randomly.

There was someone in their neighborhood who was related to the Lanza family. The term "related" in that era was a "relative" term, connected perhaps by blood, marriage, or long-time friendship from the Old Country. I recall a little girl named Nancy (a grandchild perhaps?) would occasionally visit this neighbor. We would play together during those times. One afternoon, we were at the neighbor's house. She and I wandered into the living room, where someone, perhaps her grandmother, shushed us. Mario Lanza was asleep on the couch! We sat on the floor, petrified stones. The idea of waking up a saint from South Philadelphia would banish us from ever playing together again.

His barrel chest rose and fell, so quiet his breathing, a dormant pow-
erhouse at that moment. We were mesmerized. We dared not move, but
he did. He shifted his body; a wave of dark hair fell over his half-open
eyes. He opened his eyes wider, half groggy, half sitting on the sofa. He
looked over at us and smiled. When he smiled, we were spellbound. His
charisma illuminated the atmosphere. He nodded, his handsome face
precisely the same as the image on the Mario Lanza albums my father
collected. He rolled over and resumed his nap. The two of us collapsed
in silent giggling, awed little girls beholding greatness. His presence filled
the small living room. His demeanor was so kind! I wanted him to sing
to us, confident his voice would be as handsome as he appeared in slumber, as powerful as he sounded on the albums that played in every house
in the Italian Pocket of Philadelphia. I might have made the Christian
Sign of the Cross while Nancy's grandmother shooed us outside.

Those months of mural work were months of song, tears, and laughter for a man whose life played out as Greek tragedy in his own Italian
opera. When rumors spread that Lanza's home was under the surveillance
of a developer, another chapter in the gentrification of the Bella Vista
section of South Philadelphia was waiting in the wings with a wrecking
ball. As my cousin said, *It's all about money.*

A historical marker now resides in front of one of the condominiums
that proclaims his birthplace, demolished in July 2018:

Mario Lanza (1921-1959), the beloved tenor, was born here as
Alfredo Cocozza.

Here as a boy, he learned the arias of many operas. He became a
radio, concert, record artist. After signing with MGM in 1947,
he made seven films; he had the title role in *The Great Caruso*
in 1951.

Let's step back a century. From 1880 to 1924, four million Italians migrated to the United States. Half of that population arrived between 1900 and 1910, termed The Great Migration of the early twentieth century. My maternal grandparents left the grinding poverty of Sicily, as Lanza's parents did from southern Italy. This massive influx of one ethnic group in a small Philadelphia area created a "Little Italy," the area known to include the 7th and Christian Street area. This area was second in size only to New York City's Italian section regarding physical geography. That's what I learned from my family and my neighbors. Children born and raised in this area grew up in an old world of skills, traditions, and religious practices. A faith-familiar environment where the streets were small, but hope was not.

The Italian Market still thrives in this Bella Vista section of the city, vibrant and far more diverse than the preceding three generations. Our families walked these streets and continue to support these establishments. I still hear the creaking of the two-wheeled shopping carts and the hucksters hawking their produce. The butcher shops, with the dry smell of sawdust that absorbed the slight trickles of blood, seeped from slain animals cut and ready for sale. The sawdust, sprinkled, laid down to respect those last specks of life, floor shining still in the aftermath, their altar. A "bella vista" of family-owned businesses, a way of life, a time that was not easy but spiritual and mostly loving. Traditions and trades brought from far away add comfort. For Mario Lanza and my family, then, for me later, a place of peace and caring, a lingering devotion from a different time. For Mario Lanza and my family, then, for me later, extraordinarily little change wherever there is a sense of immaculate Italian pride.

∽∾◯∾∾

St. Mary Magdalen De Pazzi Church was the first parish and baptismal site of Mario Lanza and my father's family. It is also the oldest Italian Catholic church in the United States. In the middle of the block on Montrose Street, its location is an architectural wonder in a relatively small worship space.

I gazed up at the artistry that surrounded us. My last visit here was when my aunt died in May 2012. Inspiration struck at that moment. Mario Lanza made his first singing informal debut in this very place. I glanced up at the two choir lofts overhead, one loft on top of the other. My cousin's suggestion to venture upstairs pulled me out of the pew. Ken's *You can't go up there!* ignored, I crept up the stairs. There was no sign preventing me; I stopped at the first loft, pitched higher than I perceived from floor level. I prayed as I inched myself along the stairway to the second loft. The brass organ pipes a mile high, increasing and decreasing in size, dwarfed me. The slight curve of the rail was the most likely place for Lanza to perform. That Christmas morning in 1940 was the first time the world heard him sing. The Bach-Gounod version of "Ave, Maria," sung by a nineteen-year-old, sung from a precarious sacred space, each note was caressing the narrow, high vaulted ceiling, floating angelic to the worshippers below. This young man wasn't talented. He was gifted.

The little Italian ladies swore Lanza was infused with the spirit and the voice of Enrico Caruso, who died in 1921, eight months after Lanza was born. It never took much diligence for these wonderful older women, imbued in the folklore of old wives' tales, to connect the dots of fate.

❦

Late one October afternoon in 1959, my playing outside was interrupted by seeing white floral arrangements draped in black crepe ribbon posted beside the doorbells of neighbors' houses. In the days before funeral parlors, people in the area would hang these floral pieces outside their houses to identify where mourners could pay their respects. The origin of the archaic phrase "crepehanger" might claim its roots in this practice. These were the mourning signals, attached with reverence, increasing as the minutes passed. Their appearance puzzled me; something was out of place. It was too soon for Halloween decorations. Then, with the sound of crying, I hear windows flung open, despite the autumn weather, to let the music out—Mario Lanza music.

I did not grasp the endless sight of black and white that afternoon. The neighbor who told me Mario Lanza died looked at my front door without the funeral draping and told me to tell my mother immediately.

Houses on both sides of the street with floral soldiers at the door made my own look disrespectful. I still couldn't understand it—how could Mr. Lanza be dead when I could hear him singing? Why were my parents and everyone else shocked beyond words? My six-and-a-half-year-old mind could only absorb a South Philadelphia as it plunged into darkness.

Mario Lanza died in Rome at the age of thirty-eight. A heart attack, someone wailed. Phlebitis, someone else cried out. His phenomenal achievement and crushing downfall left his parents bereft of their only child. His temperament and his talent were an entanglement in the entertainment industry. His artistry was at odds with MGM management. The demands of the silver screen, the yo-yo dieting to keep up appearances without compromising his voice, led to binge drinking. His generous heart was preyed upon by the unscrupulous, and financial difficulties deepened. Two speeds, fast and reckless, drove him. Five months later, his wife died of a respiratory ailment. Everyone said she died of a broken heart. The singing once said to be heard a block away diminished to eternal silence.

We had much to discuss during lunch with my cousin. Her block at the moment remains immune from developers. Upon her demise, she expects that her house, a corner property, will be knocked down and replaced by townhouses, just like Mario Lanza's. Her home was where my father and his siblings were born.

On Friday, January 29, 2021, Philadelphia installed signs designating the 1200 block of Reed Street as Mario Lanza Way. The virtual unveiling appears in a Podcast dated January 31, 2021, the 100th anniversary of Lanza's birth. The Philadelphia City Council adopted the resolution that the renamed street is official and permanent. Pennsylvania Governor Tom Wolf declared January 31, 2021, Mario Lanza Day.

The relocated Mario Lanza Museum opened on March 6, 2021. The fund-raisers associated with the museum will continue to assist aspiring opera singers.

Those who claim Mario Lanza as a second-rate talent should heed the three tenors of the 1990s who attribute their success to him: the renowned trio of Luciano Pavarotti, Placido Domingo, and Jose Carreras.

And from this little girl whose fascination for the Three Wise Men was set alight by Mario Lanza's version of "We Three Kings," his voice will always remain in my heart.

Cent Anni, Alfredo Cocuzzo, Rest in Peace. May the guardian angel with her shining wings forever hold your hand as you walk in Paradise.

Fidel Phobia

—◦⟨⊙⟩◦—

FLASHBACK: 1950's—The Cold War between the Soviet Union and the U.S. intensifies. Communist is the "C" word of the era, a label with a slogan, "Better Dead Than Red." Red scare phobia creates hysteria. Amorphous nightmares haunt me.

NEWS FLASH: 1959—Castro became dictator of Cuba on February 16, 1959. Jumping rope and roller skating lose their appeal. I am 6 years old, and all I know is that Cuba is very close to Florida. That's what everyone keeps saying. Castro is a Communist. Castro-phobia hovers over me and sneaks into my school uniform.

FLASH FORWARD: 1962—Today, 10/16/62, The Cuban Missile Crisis begins. Classmates during lunchtime recess say the rosary, clutching their beads instead of jumping ropes—no need for the nuns to yell us into quiet. Evening TV programming turns upside down, flashing unrelenting images of discord and unrest. Khrushchev bangs his shoe on the conference table in protest, an act that brings no laughter, only his swan song. He, the three-shoe-ed politician, does not worry me. I watch, wondering what my parents would do if I tried to bang one of my smelly shoes on the kitchen table. I smell his smelly sock from his stinky foot exposed under the table. I wonder if the men on either side of him want to clip their noses with a clothespin. Suddenly, I notice my parents seem different. I don't understand why they react so strangely to the TV; their stunned, static reaction confuses me. I watch my parents exchange word-less glances, eyes lock in a tennis match of fear. My siblings are already in bed, not part of the audience. The unseen Castro looms overall, presence absent on TV, terrifying me far more than Khrushchev's shoe tantrum.

Dad tucks me into bed. I ask him: "Dad, are we going to die?" I pull the covers close over my head. I cannot see my father. The forever pause, then he answers, "Linda, you should enjoy your childhood."

And now, I know—I *know*. He does not know. Dad never lies; he does not know. He cannot answer me. His husky-toned voice belies his words.

Dad, peerless in emergencies, peerless in telling the truth and always expecting the same from us, always adamant about doing the right thing—he was at crossroads with my question. I fear his tone of voice, a tone of thinly veiled assurance, speaking words more for his peace of mind than for mine. I take him by surprise; I place him in my despair, and my fright intensifies. I am alone. I dare not ask him again. I find no comfort or rec-onciliation as I replay our exchange in my panicky mind. His tone of voice locks inside me forever, that tone never to repeat itself. I keep it to myself. I am the oldest child. I keep this from my two siblings. I hide it from my mother to protect her. I know dad will not tell her. I know I cannot handle what she might not say if I *do* tell her. The terror I feel from Dad's words ensnares me. I struggle with whom to fear more, him or Castro.

Thirteen days of triskaidekaphobia bring daytime air raid drills and nightmares. Castro-mares of Castro flying a one-seater, open-cockpit bomber jet. A cartoon demon with a black cigar hanging from the corner of his mouth. Fierce-eyed, black-rimmed, bulging caricature eyes, laughter diabolical as he places our house in his crosshairs. Black jet engine, smoking of burnt oil and cigar ashes. I am too frightened to scream.

POV FLASH: 1971—Freshman year at Rosemont College, mid-Oc-tober. The not-so-studious among us engage in the fifteen-minute rule countdown. The College grants professors a fifteen-minute time window for arrival. Failure to do so permits the students to vacate the classroom. Someone gleefully exclaims *She is not coming!* The sound from the far end of the hallway pricks my sharp hearing. *Not so,* I reply *I hear the click of her Cuban heels!* Indeed, the click of those Cuban heels reaches the entrance of the room.

Our Spanish professor arrives. Her opening statement of the day comes from nowhere without warning. She declares, in Spanish, that Fidel Castro has sex appeal. Her smile is incendiary. Her flair for the dramatic, as always, is unsurpassed. She folds her arms across her chest as if to barricade herself from our reaction. There is raucous laughter and scathing commentary. Hearing this comment from her in Spanish is far worse than hearing it in English. It worsens as she calmly explains that her family was expulsed from their plantation without warning, everyone escaping with only the shirts on their backs. Her remarks are a test to see if our class is paying attention. Her message that power is sexy is lost on us. Those of us who feel ashamed of the callous reaction of the rest of us are dumbfounded and embarrassed. I cross my arms over my chest to ease our professor's heartbreak, to pledge my empathy for her. Sleep that night is a ten-year reunion Castro-mare. I cannot escape him. He has returned; he invades my education.

WALTERS FLASH: 2002—Barbara Walters interviews Castro on *20/20.* I do not watch the program. I hold my protest one room away from the TV. Three decades without him on my radar should make me grateful. Hardly! He is here, back *again,* like chickenpox resurrecting as shingles. I feel justified in my moratorium from this Zoster; my spouse's opinion be damned. I loudly outline what Ms. Walters will say and how Castro will respond. My husband affirms that I am right on target. He tells me he can't believe it. He can't believe I will not look at my aging nemesis. The Castro Cuban Missile Crisis nightmare reprised again, prefaced by the 1962 bedtime exchange between my father and me.

REST IN FLASHBACK: 2016—Date not needed. Castro is gone, the last cigar castrated.

RESTLESS TODAY: 2020—This very day, I free myself; no, I am never completely free of him. Childhood is not for the faint of heart.

Spitting Images

— ∘⟨∾∾⟩∘ —

My Uncle Ben was my mom's oldest brother, eleven years her senior. His birthday was June 21, so it fell on Father's Day several
times during his lifetime. Somewhere between chance and design, Father's
Day became an annual gathering celebration at Grandmom Arci's house.
There were too many of us for their small South Philadelphia home to accommodate indoors, so the backyard became a haven for the youngsters.

That yard was an Italian garden postage stamp full of flowers, plants,
and vines with a long bench attached to one side. In the far corner on
the other side was a state-of-the-art old-fashioned outhouse, a structure
of endless fascination for us kids. This outhouse was the main target for
what became the Annual Father's Day Watermelon Seed Spitting Contest.

There was never a Father's Day where I couldn't recall grandpop's annual duty of selecting a watermelon from the 9th Street Italian Market, a
few blocks from his neighborhood. In those days, the availability of fruits
and vegetables was strictly seasonal, so watermelon was our first Divine
Treat of Summer.

Grandpop was peerless in choosing the most outstanding melon in
the market's crop, so much so that the Italian dinner which preceded its
consumption was secondary to this striped treasure. We kids would bolt
through dinner and quickly beseech him to cut the object of our desire.
He willingly obliged, and with a twinkle in his eye and his firm, steady,
Sicilian hands, he would divide the melon into two gorgeous orbs of

that luscious, red-pink fruit. Before this activity, he would pause briefly, look up to Heaven, smile and say, *Ho vissuto un altro anno*, I have lived another year.

We kids charged out the back door to the yard, plates of fruit in our hands. We would line up at the bench while our uncles, fathers, and Grandpop Arci stood to our right, perfectly blocking any view from the kitchen window, allowing us to set up for our contest.

This blocked view was the ultimate ally to our shenanigans. Many years ago, my grandpop, father, and uncles fashioned a garden for grandmom built on a raised platform. It was several feet from the ground to grandmom's waist height, enabling her to fuss about her plants and flowers without any fuss. One side of the platform was attached to the wall of the kitchen window. It was an excellent vantage point for us to see nature grow and change before our eyes, not only from outdoors but from the comfortable vantage point of the windowsill inside. Grandmom hid her garden accessories in shelving under the platform, a design unique to her needs. I cannot recall another house equipped with such a charming setup.

We stuffed our faces with watermelon and attempted to spit the seeds into the outhouse toilet one by one. A tin plate attached to the top of the bowl was an even more desired target if one was available. Ah, the sound of those seedy torpedoes hitting that pan!

Pfit!!! Pfit!!! The raised garden, the men stationed in front of it, two layers of camouflage at work for us, two perfect foils for mischief! We "pftted" to our hearts' content.

The boys had an advantage. It was far more difficult for the girls to participate and not have telltale signs of watermelon juice on our Sunday dresses. I would have given anything to be able to wear shorts. In time we improved. We became far more creative than the boys.

Everyone but me, of course, clumsy Linda, my height and weight clearly at odds with the skills required. There was always some flap over who hit the target and when, with one exception.

My cousin Joanne, a petite dervish who knew no fear, outshone all of us; she could spit like a longshoreman. *Pfit! Pfit! Pfit! PING!* With lightning speed and fighter bomber accuracy, Joanne would let loose a barrage of seeds like a machine gun. God, was I envious of her.

Her talent remains unchallenged when we share reminiscences during family funerals.

 ⁓ৎ⊖ᵔ⁓

Over the past few years, my cousin Nina hosted an annual summer party. The first year of our gathering, the Annual Father's Day Seed Spitting Contest memory came up. Suddenly, those of us who were part of that memory looked at one another, nodded, got up simultaneously, grabbed a plate of watermelon, and ran into the yard, outhouse-less, but there was a wall. We set ourselves to re-enactment.

Our kids thought we had lost our minds. One of our family friends, who is like family, who knew nothing of this game but joined in, was doing very well, letting loose with a vengeance. When I asked her where this uncharacteristic, unladylike conduct came from, she looked at me, face saturated with watermelon juice, and stated, *Well, Linda, this is for all those rotten boys who wouldn't go out with me!* With that, she turned her head and shot off another round. Gripped in so much laughter, we didn't have the strength to turn on the hose to clean off the wall. We left that job to the rain.

 ⁓ৎ⊖ᵔ⁓

Learning to pick great watermelon has always been secondary to the Seed Spitting Contest. Honestly, one does not exist for me without the other. Best of all, my grandparents, mom, and aunts never knew why we wanted that aluminum pie plate so badly until many years later.

Grandpop would tell me not to worry when I saw him laughing to himself for no apparent reason. He would tell me he was laughing about a pleasant, happy memory. His sage wish for me was that his experience would become my own someday.

And so, it seems that his sage wish for me is starting to come true as I sit and think about those seed-spitting Sundays and laugh to myself and say, "I, too, have lived another year."

The Flight from the Jewelry Store

E very New Year's Day, our family visits my great-uncle Sam. It
was an annual tradition heightened because he lives on Broad
Street, South Philadelphia, above a jewelry store. An envious view of the
Mummer's Parade.

Although the number of us little visitors varies from year to year, Uncle Sam's warmth and welcome never does. My parents steer us through
the store with its impressive array of gold, silver, and jewels. Objects d'art
of various shapes and sizes adorn the surrounding area. A life-size statue
of Venus de Milo at the stairway's base leads to my uncle's quarters.

This statue never fails to unsettle me. On one occasion, I asked my
mom why Venus had no arms. Mom answered that it was a model of a
very famous statue and that it was a mystery whether the original one
had arms. I ponder this and stare at Venus. Her opaque, disinterested
stare and exquisite frame rival my curious glance and overweight body.
I develop an intense dislike for the statue. How ridiculous that anyone
would go to so much trouble to create a work of art and not add arms.

I forget Venus once I climb the stairway. Uncle Sam and other relatives greet us. Grandpop and Uncle John, Uncle Sam's brothers, herd us
into the front room.

At best, my personal feelings are mixed toward the Mummers. We live
in the shadow and the spirit of the Mummers all year round. The South
Philadelphia String Band practices at our neighborhood playground

and the elementary school, half a block from our house. The ukulele and glockenspiel produce a steady diet of sound on spring and summer nights. Girls and women are not permitted membership to any Mummer's band. A brother of one of my grade school friends triumphs over this fact. He and his male counterparts enact their parts in the band in our schoolyard to spite us.

Nyah, Nyah! NO GIRLS!! GIRLS STINK!!!

We girls huff our way to the other side of the schoolyard and imitate the boys' routine to the point of their complete exasperation. We exaggerate their footwork and mimic the sound of the instruments, *ling, ling, ling, ling, ling, ling,* which prompts punishment by some nuns for our behavior.

Although these incidents tend to dim my perception of the Mummers as a group, the idea of being at Uncle Sam's overcomes my feelings. The grown-ups assemble us at the windows opened enough to allow our hands and faces freedom of movement. There is a radiator between the windows. We can eat all the hotdogs we want. The view, the food, the cold air, the radiator, and the envious stares of the crowds on the sidewalk provide the best of all worlds. It was as if we had the privilege of breaking the law of gravity.

The smell of tobacco and pipe smoke fills the air behind us as grandpop, Uncle Sam, and Uncle John talk about news from the rest of their family in Acireale, a region of Catania, Sicily. The smoke rises in reverent Solomonic columns above them. They sit in a conference-like pose as grandmom frets about the fouled air.

The Mummers put on a spectacular show. All of Broad Street is under the spotlight with a cast of thousands. Marching feet and strumming hands. People clap and scream for their neighborhood band—all of humanity in costumes from every walk of life and description. We kids are in an element of high excitement. Mostly, there is always an adult close by to watch us.

Or almost always.

It only takes a moment for an adult to turn their head. It always seems to be the signal for pandemonium in the subconscious minds of children.

So it is New Year's Day. We take our places at the windows, our legs dangling from our chairs. I'm about seven years old. I am beside my cousin Anthony, one year older than me and at least a foot taller. He leans out the window farther than I care to venture. He has already been reprimanded about this by one of our aunts. At that moment, no one is watching.

The hotdog he is about to eat is in his right hand. He is busy yelling out the window at the next approaching band. In his excitement, he clenches both fists and cheers.

He squeezes too hard. Before I can intervene, Anthony's hotdog shoots out of its roll. It takes flight in a high arc. It tumbles with the grace of an acrobat. The mustard and relish cling to the hotdog for their lives as Anthony and I do to the windowsill.

A group of sequined Pharaohs approaches as our beef projectile continues to pirouette. A thousand thoughts hit my mind like ice water. Our fate is about to match that of Ben Hur and his family the moment the tile slips from the roof of their home and hits the Governor. My mind races:

WE WILL RUIN THE PARADE.

WE WILL BE ARRESTED.

WE WILL NEVER BE INVITED BACK TO UNCLE SAM'S.

AND THEN, THERE ARE OUR FATHERS . . .

We scream. One of the band members heard us or just happened to look up in our direction. Even from the two stories below, he sees our faces of terror. He sees the hotdog too, which is closing in on his glockenspiel. To our total amazement, he smiles and yells up at us.

Lunch!! T'ank you, guys!

The hotdog misses his instrument by half an inch and falls to the pavement. The mustard and relish decorate the curb. The young man smiled at us, played "Dem Golden Slippers," and continued up Broad Street with the rest of his group.

Anthony and I collapse with laughter and relief. My heart keeps time with the music. If I am ever to believe in my Guardian Angel, it's now. The cold air against my face is a delightful warm breeze. Naturally, we keep this incident to ourselves.

As we leave my uncle's apartment, we stop at the Venus statue to put on our hats and gloves. I glance over at her, and somehow, her face appears different. Like a betrayer, her glance is defiant and knowing. This day she is as real to me as my conscience.

Yet, she does not overpower me completely. Inner defiance drives me to do the only thing I can do. I glare at Venus, hold out my arms in an *I have something you don't have* pose, and stick my tongue out at her.

We grow up. Some traditions continue; others do not. Uncle Sam dies. Anthony joins the Mummers. He becomes a Quaker City String Band member who always places high in the contest standings. They are always terrific. He played the saxophone for twenty-five years until his death in 2011. He was one big guy who knew how to keep his feathers numbered and always watched out for flying hotdogs. I gave him a copy of this memory during our last visit, our final meeting. His laughter and tears as he read these words will live with me forever.

The Gift of the Immigrant

(Note: The names of the characters are fictional.)

There were seventy-six of us in a one-doored fourth-grade classroom. Sister Gerald ran this class with an iron hand.

Back then, most Catholic churches were solidly ethnic. Ours was an Italian parish in a rough neighborhood. Our church was beautiful, but the parish was of modest means, comprised of large families with small incomes. We lived in narrow row houses, a narrowness that sometimes affected our attitudes.

Attitudes that did not end at the adult level. But I'm getting a little ahead of myself.

It was October. I was one of the biggest kids in the class. My height earned me the seating privilege of the last desk, the fifth row. The handles of the ancient vinyl accordion coat closet met at the back of my chair, a daily torment. The Class Pest, the last seat at the far-left corner of the room, would unhinge it from the top, kicking it at a whim. He kicked it one day when I stood up to read. The dilapidated door hit me. Sister Gerald, sitting at her desk, frowned. All she heard was a commotion.

Got you thisss time, Messina! said the Class Pest. My eyes narrowed. *Leave me alone.*

Back then, no boy would call a girl by her first name and vice versa. That meant you were "in love" with that person, destined to marry. Far worse than accusing someone of having cooties. No love or cooties lost here. I detested the Class Pest.

Sister Gerald lumbered down the aisle. Our sardine-packed rows of children made this act a challenge. She was small, rotund, and old. Her habit and lopsided gait gave her the appearance of an overgrown penguin, with one more outstanding feature.

Sister had a body odor that could part an aisle faster than Moses could part the Red Sea. She descended on us and stamped her foot.

You bold and brazen articles! What is the meaning of this?

I scrambled from her deafening fumes, colliding with the standing half of the closet. It careened on its track, done so easily after years of child abuse. The class cackled. Suddenly, one boy stood up and told her that the Class Pest had caused the incident.

This classmate, Gallagher, was one of the only Irish kids in the school. Memory has it that our pastor allowed his family to join the parish as they lived across the street from our parish. Perhaps the real reason was that Gallagher's father was an electrician. The pastor placed him on call for every maintenance issue. It was quite a suitable arrangement. His children were as rough as any of us, making ethnic squabbles rare. Gallagher protecting me was nothing for him to fear.

Sister promptly blistered the Class Pest's left hand with the metal-edged ruler. She spared his right hand for his written punishment; *I will obey Sister Gerald,* scrawled one hundred times on loose-leaf paper in Palmer Method handwriting.

Shortly after this incident, our school prepared for the arrival of the Cardinal. Sister drilled us for weeks on our catechism. This visit coincided with the arrival of a new family to the parish—the Di Bello family. The Di Bello's were from Sicily, with a child in nearly every grade. None of the children spoke English.

The day Catarina came to our class, Sister did the only thing she could do. She placed her with me. *I need you to take care of Catarina,* she said.

Inwardly, I groaned. My classmates snickered behind Sister's back. Then, I saw Catarina. She was tall, slim, beautiful, and easily four years older than me. Her hair was dark and straight; her eyes were hazel-green, exotic. Hers was a woman's face from a Renaissance painting. I thought of my mother's immigrant parents. I couldn't refuse. I agreed for their sake; I agreed because Sister's proximity over-saturated my olfactory nerve. Catarina sat next to the desk beside me, so tall her knees lifted the desk from the floor.

∾◦⊙◦∿

The Cardinal came while Sister was taking attendance, her most torturous daily chore. This Irish nun had no patience with Italian surnames. Her pronunciations grated like fingernails on a chalkboard. Gallagher's name was a relief.

Her verbal stumbling was not lost on the Cardinal. When Gallagher was roll-called, the Cardinal questioned him, then asked him to repeat his name.

He proudly replied *I am Thomas Gallagher, Grade 4, student of Sister Gerald's class of the Odor of St. Joseph.*

Sister was too busy beaming to realize Gallagher's innocent slip. It wasn't lost on the class or the Cardinal. The Cardinal controlled his facial muscles, thanked Gallagher, and moved on. The story spread through the school in a flash. Gallagher's phrase was Sister Gerald's new calling card.

Catarina struggled with her new environment, the language barrier, and homesickness. Our classmates were another story. Most of them were no help at all. It baffled me how people could treat Catarina as an outcast, as most of us could trace our ancestry to the same homeland. Their meanness was almost devastating; they called her stupid or pretended she wasn't there.

∾◦⊙◦∿

And then there was the incident in the girls' lavatory.

One day, I recall standing in the lavatory waiting for Catarina; something was amiss. She seemed to be in the bathroom longer than usual. I began to worry. One girl decided to crawl under Catarina's stall. Suddenly, there was a scream.

Catarina's bleeding, she taunted, wriggling from the cubicle. Her nasty friends chimed in. Catarina emerged, mortified. My immediate thought was the discussion my mom and I had after viewing a recent program on TV about hemophilia. It surprised me to learn that it was rare in women. Catarina's bleeding was too much for me to handle. *Catarina has hemophilia,* which was too frightening to imagine. I was furious with my classmates. I took Catarina by the hand and walked with her to the schoolyard. Nearly ill with fear, I resolved to protect her. I was on a mission.

꧁꧂

Christmas was coming. Sister consented to a Pollyanna, the first and last one she would ever hold. I explained this to Catarina; she seemed to understand. Catarina understood more and more as the days passed. Her English improved with timid steadiness. A shy friendship developed between us.

It was the day before Christmas Eve. It was "dress up" day. Mom reminded me to walk like a lady, my venture with nylon stockings was a new experience. My legs were already itching with their unexpected contact with hosiery—my first steps to womanhood. I kissed mom goodbye and packed my gift in my school bag. I couldn't wait to find out who had me for Pollyanna.

The classroom was in a fracas. Sister's attempt at an organized gift exchange went for naught. Students tossed wrapping paper and bows everywhere. Her command for order went unheeded.

There were games, toys, and dolls. The Class Pest received a wind-up fire engine that sputtered about the floor. Christmas carols blared from the public address system. I waited. Sister called my name at last and handed me a package.

It was flat and square. Everyone was curious. The Class Pest smirked. *What could that be? It looks like a fire engine!* I ignored him. The other kids pressed forward. The chain reaction, everyone's pushing, caused the coat closet to sway. My peripheral vision spied the Class Pest unhooking the right side.

My unwrapped package distracted me. I was stunned; my gift of two coloring books was revealed. I looked up, saw Catarina, and realized *she* was my gift giver. Our classmates howled in derision. The books slipped to the floor. One of the books opened. In horror, Catarina and I noticed pages scribbled with crayons. One of her sisters had taken liberties with my gift. Some creep grabbed my books, tearing several pages, creating coloring book confetti. Catarina's mortification was complete.

The Class Pest struck again. He waved his pricey gift with pomp, chanting *stupid!* at her. I moved to her side. I warned him to leave her alone. He whirled into my face; *Hey, Fatso Messina, I'm not talking to you!*

He swung the fire engine in a slow arc. Catarina sobbed. I warned him again to leave her alone. He feigned submission; he loosened his grip on his toy. He pulled at my curls, saying, *Messina, even your curls are fat!* The boys bellowed. The Class Pest moved to take a bow.

As he threw up his arms to bask in glory, the fire engine flew into the air destined for Catarina's temple. I remembered the lavatory incident. Catarina. Hemophilia. My mind locked itself in terror.

THAT DID IT.

I pulled myself to full height. I was in front of the Class Pest. It was as if I were seeing him for the first time. With unaccustomed anger as red as his fire engine, I pushed him with all my might.

The Class Pest hit the coat closet hard, and part of the outer frame collapsed. He now saw me for the first time. His eyes showed the truth. *He was afraid of me.* It was a thrill I have never forgotten.

The fire engine narrowly missed Catarina. When it hit the floor, the Class Pest and I scrambled for it. I retrieved it. Then, there was Sister Odor and her voice. *Anna Messina, what is going on?!*

Sister startled me. I dropped the fire engine. It rolled down my leg, creating a tire tread runner in my brand-new stockings. All I thought of was that after Sister killed me, mom would. Catarina wailed. Sister learned what happened. The Class Pest had both hands blistered with the metal-edged ruler. The color of his hands matched his gift. I kept quiet.

Sister lectured us on the true meaning of Christmas. I felt her scolding aimed at me. I was miserable. Catarina took my hand and apologized. I was too embarrassed and confused to cry. At that moment, I saw Catarina for who she was. My heart went out to her. Some kids felt guilty and started speaking to her like a human being.

∽◦⊙◦∾

We moved the following Spring. I found out Catarina was tested and placed in the seventh-grade class. She proved to be extremely bright.

Soon, my maturing process taught me that Catarina wasn't a hemophiliac. Perhaps my classmates' treatment toward her was *their* fear of being perceived as "backward," perceptions once endured by their grandparents.

I still think of Catarina every Christmas. And the Class Pest. And Gallagher.

And Sister Gerald of the Odor of St. Joseph.

If I Had One Wish

⸺◦✺◦⸺

There are more moments than I care to admit when I wish I could go back in time to speak with my grandparents. If I were only permitted one question, without hesitation, I would ask my grandmother why she said this to me:

Leenda, what's-a right is a wrong-a; what's-a wrong-a is a right-a.

We were alone in her living room one day. Grandmom was mending; I was reading. Every so often, I stopped reading and watched her at work. Hands were always in motion. At one point, she broke away from her contented gaze and dropped her needlework on her lap.

Her face turned serious when she stated those words. It startled me. I couldn't have been more than fourteen years old. Other than this remark, nothing else about her seemed out of the ordinary.

Philosopher Sidelined

Leenda, Leenda!
What-sa wrong-a/is-a right-a!
What-sa right-a/is-a wrong-a!

Wrong-a/Right-a
Right-a/Wrong-a
Criss-a/cross-a/song-a.

What was behind those phrases?
What caused such ominous words
so somber   unlike her
so cheerful but reserved?

Absurd to my outspoken ear
mind self-absorbed its match
such simple words in a twisted phrase
supplanted my young mind
unfazed.

Why was it said to me alone?
those words   her tone unblurred,
why was it even said   at all?
me, smug and
worldly heard.

Perhaps I was not meant to know
this outburst mystery—
no sooner said   her robust laugh
turned to the gravy pot
her kitchen wisdom stirred the meal—
I never knew her prompt.

Her thoughts ran deep   her sewing
threaded knowledge day and night
I never paused to think about
her needlework of life.

Then came that one
Eureka day,
when insight did alight—
That day, words once
had made no sense
Resurrected! Aha!
Why, Grandmom, dear Grandmom,
How is it you were right?

Instead of pondering everywhere
of moments lost
of journeys crossed—
two generations   now I see
simply just look into me.

I let go of
that need to know
Life is unfair
and that's enough—
I feel you smiling
from above,
I coil onto your Wisdom tight:

Oh, Grandmom, dear Grandmom,
Sage Woman, you were right!

Pot It's Not

———⚬⟨⚬⟩⚬———

One of the best stories about my Grandfather that I keep in my mind today so that I don't cry is one of innocence turned to hilarity. One of his great pleasures, and talents, was that he possessed a green thumb. I would refer to it as his "Italian Brown Thumb" because his complexion was somewhat tan. His hands, in particular.

There wasn't a seed that refused to grow for him. When he came to live with us, my father and uncles made a small garden patch for him at the side of our house. Every inch yielded vegetables, plants, and flowers. His true favorites were the Italian herbs: oregano, parsley, basil, and rosemary. His summer harvest yielded far more than we and our neighbors needed in their fresh-grown state, so he decided to dry the herbs and bottle them for use during cold weather. The herbs that dried best were the oregano and the basil. He methodically and deliberately cut the herbs, washed them gently, then strung each leaf with needle and thread in long strands. He would hang them on the clothesline rigged up from our garage door to the end of our driveway.

The neighborhood kids knew exactly how it looked and what it resembled. The rumor spread, and by then, grandpop was Grandpop Arci to the entire neighborhood. It was the mid-1970s. Finally, when I could no longer stand it, I told him why he would see the kids pointing at the clothesline, waving at him, and giving him the thumbs-up sign. He

roared with laughter when he realized the kids were saying he was growing and drying "pot" outside the house!

No one ever touched his leaves of temptation, but once grandpop
acquired this knowledge, the bumper crop increased one hundredfold.
And so today, when I went to the cemetery, I took ground basil and
oregano, rubbed it across his name on the gravestone (which runs the
entire horizontal width of its surface), and placed some at the angel's
tombstone feet. Then, I spread more of his earthly delight at my parents',
aunts', and uncles' graves. My tears were bittersweet. I cried against my
will, but these were tears of gratitude and unity. He was and is so greatly
loved and is so very dearly missed. Maybe some bold seeds will take root.

I won't worry. The St. Denis cemetery is full of Italians. Please keep
my secret safe.

Pulp Slicktion

———❦———

That last Thanksgiving, Grandpop Arci and I sought out a new food adventure, making pumpkin pie from scratch.

Pumpkin was an enigma for him, strange as it sounds. Grandpop was an outstanding cook, his range of expertise with vegetables was peerless, yet this gourd had never met his acquaintance.

So that Saturday morning, when he saw me lugging a misshapen Cinderella reject through our front door, his curiosity got the better of him. He announced, rolling up his sleeves and grinning, that he would be happy to work with me in gutting the pumpkin.

He was seated at the kitchen table, a walking cane perched on the end of the chair. I arranged the cutlery before him. He inspected the knives and the other accessories needed to begin our task.

This pumpkin was an unwieldy, bottom-heavy beast. Grandpop quickly realized this, steadying it as I cut through what would be his first assignment. Slowly, we worked together. I stopped midway and turned the other side of the pumpkin toward me to complete the cutting. As I did so, I realized much of the weight came from the juice and seeds inside the gourd. I proceeded with caution.

That's when my efforts took a nosedive. I lost control of the knife, and the pumpkin flew off the table. It smacked against the kitchen island, ricocheted under the table, and split into three misshapen sections.

Before I could drop to the floor to survey the damage, grandpop moaned, *Leenda, I'm slipping!* Parts of the pumpkin slammed against his shoes, juice, and seeds waxed around them, and his reflex to extricate himself slid him into pulpy quicksand.

We were in a deadlocked struggle. Grandpop's cane teetered and plunked to the floor, out of my immediate reach. Grandpop's chair was moving against our will. No one else was home; I could see where this was leading. My only option was to flatten myself along the floor; in doing so, I stretched with all my might for the cane. I don't know how I managed to maneuver it against the kitchen wall while I spread myself across the floor, grabbing grandpop's shoes, telling him to push back to the wall while I held on.

Suddenly, he started to laugh; this variable added a new pitch to my rescue plan. *Dear God, help me out of this*, I prayed. I pushed him and the chair with all my might, moving him out of danger. He was still laughing. I stood up, covered with the squashed squash. The seeds beaded themselves in a necklace down the front of my sweatshirt. The tears in my eyes weren't only from laughter and relief but an unspoken realization that we might never have a chance to do this again.

Grandpop's observation, still with a grin on his face, was, *See that, Leenda, we're never too old to learn new t'ings!*

I don't remember how the pumpkin pie turned out or how many seeds I continued to find for weeks afterward. Still, that narrow escape and those words of wisdom have never been more accurate for me than it was for Cinderella when her pumpkin turned into her enchanted carriage.

The Last Tangle in South Philadelphia

———⁕∞⁕———

The first thing all Italians learn in utero is never to refute Italian Old Wives' Tales.

My mother experienced retching heartburn when she was pregnant with my sister. Her mother, the matriarch of the IOWT group in her neighborhood, prophesied that this ailment was a sure sign that her daughter would bear a child with a full head of hair.

Indeed, my sister came into the world with the thickest head of dark brown hair I have yet to see on any other human infant. I clearly remember her arrival (I was five-and-a-half years old). Those yester years of watching "The Lone Ranger" had me thinking that mom arranged my sister's appearance through Tonto, the Lone Ranger's Native American Guide.

———⁕∞⁕———

My paternal grandmother died in 1989. My first thought that came to mind at her wake was that even at 91, she still possessed a full head of hair. For the first time, I also noticed that my hairline is exactly like hers, even to that one section on the upper right side that has what our family calls a juffe (clump) of unruly waviness. This juffe still skirts my efforts at combing as a matador does with a bull in an arena.

Grandmom's wake occurred in her neighborhood, close to where she lived with my aunt and her family. The funeral home was regarded as a neighborhood institution, meaning, of course, ethnicity by all matters of appearance.

But this place was unlike one I had ever seen before or since. It was very narrow. It seemed it couldn't decide whether it wanted to be a funeral home, an auction house, or a furniture store. There were chattels of every description, arranged in various groupings, enough to challenge the mind of a sober person who couldn't recall if they drank too much before arriving to pay respects.

This funeral home also had an upper floor. Halfway up the stairway was a red neon sign that flashed "EXIT," prompting someone's four-year-old cousin to ask if God was *up there.*

Initially, we stood with our parents in the grieving line. The limited space forced us to separate from them. We moved to the opposite side of the room, toward the end of the building. We sculpted ourselves around the ornate pieces of art and the furnishings, expecting to hear calls for biddings any minute.

True to form, no Italian funeral home would be complete without a mantle. Nor would it be acceptable without Renaissance bric-a-brac perched on the top of its ledge.

My sister chose this spot to flag down our cousins for a separate impromptu reunion. In a matter of moments, she had us laughing. As I stood opposite her, the strangest feeling overcame me that something didn't seem right.

My sister has a terrific eye for expensive, beautiful things. Mutual attraction lurked nearby.

Stark terror hit me when I realized her hair enmeshed itself on the mantel's masterpiece, her chuckling nods innocently luring it to a five-foot plunge of certain fragmented death to the realm of the floor. I shrieked at her not to move. I grabbed her arm; I assumed this entrapped object d'art was priceless. I cautiously extricated her hair from this figurine of a young man and woman in formal nineteenth-century attire in a dance pose. The woman's springtime dress arrayed in a fan, full-floating, floral, and breezy. The man in an evening suit, bowing politely, barely touching her hand, the pair about to begin their pas de deux to silent music.

Unraveling my sister's ensnared tresses was like trying to disengage a tripwire. Above us, the "EXIT" sign, still flashing red, admonished us. My fingers twitched in agitation and suppressed hysteria. My cousins remained on the lookout for the funeral director, who would have every right to embalm us on the spot had he caught us in the act.

We grandchildren could barely contain our laughter, losing complete control in the relief of the moment of disentanglement. All mom saw was her misconceived perception of disrespect. She resurrected the *Don't-Make-Me-Tell-Your-Father* look that smote fear in us when we were kids.

To make matters worse, the presiding priest decided to pray the Rosary. We still could not calm down, which sunk us further from mom's good graces. It took quite a while for her to let her guard down and forgive us. Grandmom, from her place of eternal reward, must have distracted her son from the commotion. Thank God my mother remained silent.

We grandkids knew without a doubt that our grandmother was roaring with laughter with the angels in Heaven. If it weren't for her divine intervention, it would have been the last tangle for all of us.

Sewing Vest with Many Buttons

I might have saved myself a lot of time if I had saved that old vest and just sewed buttons on it to keep an organized track of my stash. Now that I think of it, I still have an old one. One of my MFA classmates suggested I repurpose it for my collection. Hmmm. The possibilities for organization are endless. I could divide the vest into quadrants, front and back. Sew the plain, semi-translucent white ones for cuffs and others of similar design on the back. Sew plain black buttons there too. Maybe even use safety pins rather than fool with the constant cutting of thread for each one. The front top quadrants could be for fancy buttons on one side and larger vibrant ones on the other. The lower quadrants could be set aside for novelty buttons, ones that look like objects/animals/flowers, for accessories or specialty items.

I've always had a passion for buttons, miniature works of art, and whimsical shapes, that touch that sets an ordinary outfit apart from the rest. Such a small object with an extensive history, the oldest button was first discovered in the Indus Valley (now Pakistan), dating back 5000 years. Its composition in the early days of its history was that of a curved shell. Initially, these knobby pieces were ornamentation. That changed in the 13th century when clothing made in Germany included the button to close garments. The trend spread quickly through Europe from that time onward. Button lockets were made to store compasses during World Wars I and II.

Not all buttons are created equal. The most common are flat, with two or four holes in them. The shank button has a holed notch on its back for the thread to hold it in place. There are stud buttons, usually on blue jeans and other denim items. These are riveted, with a button on one side and a disc on the other. There are covered buttons made of metal notched with teeth to hold the fabric in place, which is very common on wedding gowns.

Buttons are made of natural and manufactured materials. Thinking outside of the button for a moment, think of phrases that contain the word: button-up, button your lips, pushing someone's buttons, cute as a button, buttonhole someone, hitting the panic button. When my father would become impatient, my mother would say that he was making buttons. The word itself might be derived from the French word "bouton."

Buttons in Italian culture were sacred items. My grandmother would sometimes crochet a button into a scarf or a doily; very feminine, very *her*. If I were lucky and found a seashell with a naturally crafted hole, I'd follow my grandmother's lead. To this day, if I lose an earring, its mate becomes a button/pin on a jacket or a cloth handbag.

It was fascinating that buttons took a divergent path in 1861 when the first political button was made for Abraham Lincoln when he ran for president. His image was set with a ferrotype, a primitive photograph of tin and lacquer. The rest was button history. The button that achieved the most fame was the yellow smiley face button that debuted in the 1960s. I remember its first appearance; we high school students couldn't get enough of them. Those yellow faces spread like a virus! Thinking about this is making me smile now. I thank my MFA classmate, Watsuki Harrington, for this idea. I think I will repurpose that old vest, who knows what stories might appear on its cloth!

A Promise and *The Pieta*

‑∽⊙∾‑

Imust have been no more than eight or nine years old when the buzzing began about the possibility that some famous statue in Rome might come to the New York World's Fair of 1964-1965. The buzzing became a rumbling. My mother spoke of the news with great excitement. I asked a million questions. *Where was Rome? Why all the fuss?* I couldn't understand why this should be so important. Mom tried to explain it. I kept looking at a picture of two figures chiseled out of marble. Both my grandmothers' copies held the same reverence. The TV ran a program about it, some show for grown-ups. And an extensive newspaper article, words printed around that same picture. *What was this about?* I thought *It's only a statue.* As time passed, I understood this wasn't just any statue. It was *The Pieta* by Michelangelo, who was considered a saint in Italian culture. As updates hit the press, my mother followed the statue's every move.

∽⊙∾

In August 2019, my husband and I visited Rome. On that lovely Saturday evening, as we searched for a church that might celebrate Mass at the twilight hour, we came upon the Santi Dodici Apostoli, the Church of the Twelve Apostles. The church, dedicated in the sixth century to the original followers of Jesus, contains the remains of Saints James and Philip. We were amazed to discover that this was the parish of Michelangelo.

We hastened our steps and entered the church. We read from the placard in the vestibule that the building was completed in 1714. We seated ourselves at a side altar, the location for Mass that evening. I couldn't maintain a reverent posture; my curiosity was immediately piqued. There was enough time to walk through the three naves, to stare at the Corinthian columns. I realized the possibility that a work of Michelangelo might be located here. We learned later that the marble tombs to the right of the high altar are attributed to his artistry.

I resumed my place at the side altar. This space was diminutive by comparison, shadowy, and peaceful. Several modest pews faced the altar. Laminated worship aids, meant to assist visitors in following the ceremony, were printed in Italian. The priest's Italian words sounded comforting. The words of this Romance language translated easily for me as I read the prayer aid. My study of Latin and Italian heritage provided me with an advantage. I understood a few words of the priest's sermon: *patiencia* (patience), *grazia* (grace), *forza d'animo* (fortitude), the rhythm, the cadence, and the trace of the scented lit candles so welcoming.

I must admit that my eye and mind did not focus entirely on the priest's rituals. As I gazed at the angels who seemed to float across the vaulted ceiling, I could not dismiss the thought of Michelangelo. Could he have sat where I was sitting? Did dust from his sculpture work leave their remnants in this pew? Perhaps he and I have studied these very walls, these frescoes surrounding me, a half-millennium later. My thoughts held with no understanding of his process, unmatched by Michelangelo's brilliance. I felt sure that he, as I did, raised his eyes upwards to angels hovering over us, guarding the vaulted ceiling, that temporary heaven.

Did Michelangelo gain inspiration from the work of the titans that surrounded him? Did his fingernails trace an idea along the edge of his pew, perhaps an abstract thought, some puzzle solved? Did he pray that his labor not be risked by fierce competition in a world where reputation was as tenuous as an artist's most recent success? Did his contemporaries dwell here in prayer, perchance to beseech the saints for a vestige of his talent? Are the masterworks that surrounded us eternal? What does it mean to conquer finite space, to lead the eye upward to the feat of the artistry, to the Divine?

I smiled to myself at the thought of a master suffering a stroke of weariness, a slip of the brush on his fresco, a slightly irreverent swatch of an impulsive act so far removed from the ground on his scaffold. Who could tell from an acre of space below?

In this church, I thought of my mother, a devout, loving Catholic who would have revered this place as no other. Before departing, I lit two candles before the Blessed Mother statue; her downcast gaze seemed to steal a glance upward at me as I prayed for my deceased mother, Mary.

In 1962, Pope John XXIII granted permission to admit *The Pieta* to the fair. After his passing in 1963, his successor, Pope Paul VI, oversaw the plan's execution. After months of deliberation, the sculpture set sail from Naples, Italy, to New York City on April 2, 1964. Six million dollars insured the eight-day voyage across the Atlantic Ocean.

This masterpiece had never left Vatican City in the 465 years since its placement in St. Peter's Basilica. Extraordinary precautions were used to transport *The Pieta* to the United States.

After an eight-day voyage, it arrived in New York, unharmed, set on a marble base in The Vatican Pavilion. It was a momentous achievement, a first-time exhibit of a Michelangelo sculpture in the United States.

The Vatican Pavilion became the focal point of the fair, with its chapel supporting a golden peaked roof. Countless masterpieces adorned its walls. I have no memory of these works of art, but I'm sure none could dare approach the domain of *The Pieta*, some calling it "The Crown Jewel." It was one of the premier attractions, second in attendance rank at twenty-seven million visitors, outpaced by the General Motors Pavilion's twenty-nine million. It was the most popular international exhibit. In 1965, Pope Paul VI, the first pope to travel to the U.S., visited the Pavilion and *The Pieta* as part of his trip to the United Nations.

The venue's tremendous success was stellar but never to be repeated. Although Michelangelo's work arrived home intact in 1965, this temporary relocation caused controversy. I'd conjecture risk and expense as primary concerns. The Pope ruled that *The Pieta* would never leave the Basilica again.

My mother was ecstatic to learn we would have the opportunity to see The Vatican exhibit. A classmate's girl scout troop planned to run a one-day trip to the fair. Mom's delight over our invitation to accompany them still beats deeply in my heart.

As I reflect on that day, herding a group of eleven-year-old girls through a New York city spectacle could have been quite challenging. Large crowds and constricted lines stunned us. We were remarkably well-behaved, considering the three-hour bus ride and the two-hour wait in the sun.

The Linda-child saw it this way:

It was so hot standing in that line. I couldn't see much of anything. We were thirsty. We tried playing "I Spy," but after saying, *I spy tall/short/ little/big people walking by* repeatedly, we ran out of what we could spy. A few of us played hand-clapping games, singing, "A sailor went to sea, sea, sea//To see what he could see, see, see," and "Pease Porridge Hot," and other nursery rhymes. When we decided to change hand clap partners and moved out of our place in line, some of our mothers glared at us. The glare said *You are Girl Scouts!*

Our early arrival was advantageous. The line to enter the pavilion moved at a respectful pace. I think my mind's ear hears groups of visitors praying the rosary. I can see the prayer beads in their hands, in a set of five decades, clasped by a crucifix. Their voices intone the *Hail Mary* en route to a pilgrimage.

Stepping into an oval-shaped building was a new experience for me. My mother took my hand; the sweat of the day and the anticipation remained fresh in my mind. I visualize our stepping into a darkened corridor. Mom's breath was in my ear; she squeezed my hand in time with her heartbeat. Security measures fell somewhere between benign and non-existent, other than the omnipresent uniformed guards. I picture us walking into progressive darkness; as the lighting diminished, a low, solemn Gregorian chant emanated from the atmosphere. As the guided path continued, we narrowed our steps. Volunteers directed us to one of four (perhaps six or more) horizontal moving tracks, tiered, elevated lanes, each lane operating at a steady, deliberately slow movement. We moved past the sculpture in an embrace of stark midnight blue-blackness; we were a moving sidewalk. Did the scent of incense fill the air? Am I imagining stronger incense burnings of sweet-scented gum and spice ash, or is this my conjuring of a sacred interlude? Perhaps holy water fonts would be stationed at the exit doors.

The view was optimal for everyone. The deep blue backdrop and the four hundred lights behind and above the statue made the protecting floor-to-ceiling plexiglass seem non-existent and ethereal. The music added dignity and remembrance, a quiet, solemn pitch that kept the visitor in hushed awe. There is a vivid image of mirrors or some approximation of reflection in my pre-teen mind's eye, for I still see *The Pieta* from every angle, all at once, luminous, whole, incandescent.

My first thoughts might have been immature about the sight before me. All I remember or suspect are words of quiet reflection. Mary, Jesus' mother, eyes lowered in an eternal grief gaze; pure marble gleams pure light, pure love, pure heartbreak—pure sorrow. Sorrow. The word *pieta* means pity or compassion, yet sorrow seems more apt. That day, sorrow told me I imagined a single tear lingering on Mary's face. That day, sorrow allowed me to envision what was in Mary's mind and heart. Her heart held the memory of the angel Gabriel's visit to the birth of her Son. Her mind held the thought that this moment, captured in marble, awaited her. It led me to see her kiss her infant son for the first time, kissing the Face of God. That this exquisite rendering of exquisite sorrow set Michelangelo to capture mother and son in the serene, ageless, youthful purity. If the moving track had stopped, I would have waited for Jesus to lift his head ever-so-slightly to breathe one last time in his mother's arms. It seemed to be a distinct possibility.

∽∾⊙∾∽

It was Michelangelo's genius to retain Mary's youth in his tableaux of Holy Mother and Son. It met with little scrutiny. No Catholic I know has ever disputed her youthful depiction. As a child, Mary's young face appealed to me. Every holy card, Christmas stamp, or other representation in my memory portrays her as a young woman, humble and innocent. Eyes cast downward, always.

I've wondered how Michelangelo kept his focus during the two years he devoted to *The Pieta*. I've pondered if he hummed Gregorian Chant, the monophonic liturgical music of the Roman Catholic Church, played in the Vatican Pavilion, still sung in Latin (and in English). Maybe he sang local festive songs when he was tired of this plainchant. Perhaps, if he prayed, he prayed in modulation to his movements, quick prayers for quick strokes, fervent prayers for more demanding maneuvers. Maybe, if he prayed, a prayer of gratitude when he released the trapped figures he knew were buried within the quarried stone before him.

Perhaps this is perfect fiction or truth as I recall from my memory an account of the artist's protecting his beloved masterpiece. Michelangelo diverged from his usual practice of not signing his work when someone intentionally told a group of admirers that another sculptor had created *The Pieta*. This disconcerting remark led him to rectify the situation. Soon after this event, he secured himself in the chapel. With candlelight and chisel, he inscribed this message across the diagonal band of Mary's garment:

Michaelangelus Bonarotus Florentinus Faciebat
(Michelangelo Buonarotti, Florentine, made this)

A light touch, the lettering plain, delicate. Modest. Perfect. Risk of damaging flawlessness. He later regretted this act of pride, vowing never to repeat it.

No other sculpture Michelangelo carved created such a visceral reaction as *The Pieta*. That he would complete his masterpiece at the age of twenty-four is mystifying. How could he, hardly matured to adulthood, extract such a complex work from one large abstract block of marble? I want to believe it was perfect timing for this young man. He was not just talented but *gifted*. He, not yet jaded by what might follow in his remaining sixty-four years, what accident or curse of toil might have diminished what had to be immaculate perfection. His young, uncompromising mind holds his ideal conception and will survive the ages to eternity. I wonder if he would have done anything differently had he known his statue would be transported forty-five hundred miles across the ocean.

Out of the corner of my eye, I think I see mom's lips moving, her eyes teary. No rosary beads in hand, perhaps praying just the same. The exit ramp neared. I turned my back toward *The Pieta* to savor my last sight of the beloveds and stave off the intrusive world for one final moment before we rejoined the racket outside.

I don't remember us discussing our experience. If mom had worn a church chapel veil in the pavilion that day, that would not surprise me. That possibility comforts me.

Years passed. Mom saw no reason why she and dad couldn't take a trip to Rome. Their parental obligations to their children met, she would occasionally broach the subject to him. Dad's response would range from shrugged shoulders to, *We'll see.*

In 2002, our parish, St. Matthew's, in Northeast Philadelphia, celebrated its 75th anniversary. The parish planned a twelve-day trip to Italy for any parishioner who wished to go and had the means to do so to commemorate this milestone. My husband and I saw this as a prime opportunity for my parents (at last!) to accompany us. All appeared satisfactory until the itinerary was explained at the preliminary meeting. Seven cities and towns within ten days, Rome included. It was mostly walking tours.

My parents listened. No words needed. Too strenuous, dad stated, and don't forget mom's vertigo issue. Mom never lamented our departing without her. She left an upbeat welcome home message on our phone. I still hear every nuance of every word she spoke. We shared every moment of our excursions with our parents. We brought them every Italian religious memento we could find. We gave them a personalized, embossed written blessing from Pope John Paul II.

Had we thought about what the weather might bring, this unrealized dream would probably not have materialized. We never considered that June 2002 would be one of Italy's hottest recorded temperature months. On the day we visited Florence, the temperature hit 102 degrees. Old cities (Florence, Rome, Ravenna), old roads, and uneven walkways made the searing heat more intense. Travel of this magnitude for my parents, in their mid-seventies, might have exceeded their limits of physical exertion. Their decision might have prevented later health issues.

The situation did not relieve the unspoken guilt that permeated in me throughout our trip. The guilt will never subside completely. I now perceive early mishaps that I could have corrected. The most obvious solution would have been for one of us to accompany mom to Rome during a more temperate, less crowded season. This resolution could have surfaced had I realized sooner the root causes of dad's lack of pursuit: his flying phobia and untreated clinical anxiety. I overlooked his myriad excuses and mom's acquiescence in so many now-obvious situations. I felt I had not kept a promise to my mother. Unwittingly I, with a bachelor's degree in Psychology, disgraced myself.

Seeing *The Pieta* on that 2002 church trip dredged up unexpected irony. On that June afternoon, we waited for the crowds to diminish. Even then, we were bumped at every angle by the crush of humanity, relentless elbowing, and camera jostling. Its relocation could account for part of the buffeting. After Laszlo Toth assaulted the sculpture with twelve hammer strikes in 1972, it was moved to an alcove in St. Peter's Basilica, in the far-right corner from the front entrance of the building. The bulletproof glass was added as it had been in the Vatican Pavilion. This precaution and the corner's inherent structure present an additional limitation, causing near claustrophobia, a compression effect from approaching and departing viewers.

The 2019 visit to the Vatican was far more of a travesty. My husband and I saw swarms of tourists storm *The Pieta* that hot Sunday, August afternoon. Several groups tangled themselves in what they considered an approximation of a line. Scrambling for order, one of the guides raised a flagpole, the kind used on a golf course. He raised it high above the mob, its blood-red flag in a vehement wave, to collect his dispersed group as they collided with one another. No sooner regrouped, they surged past Mary and Jesus. Their chattering, noisy presence was a frenzy of disrespect. Barely a glimpse was seen of the Capstone of Christian Faith. This Capstone became a sideshow, a mortification.

My anger over this scene still stuns me. I reasoned not to expect my reverence as gospel behavior that everyone should follow. It stupefies me that the Vatican placed *The Pieta* in the perfect spot that enabled such crowd mentality. Without the lives of Jesus and Mary, without their promises kept, the Vatican, the governing center of the Roman Catholic Church, would not exist. Christianity—a non-entity. Jesus, Mary, and Michelangelo deserved better.

When someone tripped over me, I realized that I felt closer to this calm and perfect miracle when I saw it at the New York World's Fair than I did standing in its home base. It wouldn't be far off the mark to speculate that it was because I was with mom for the first time. I can still feel her closeness to me, our closeness to each other. Her right arm nudged my left arm, protecting me from the pressing crowd, her small, delicate fingers seeking my own. They nestled themselves in the palm of her firstborn. I sensed but could not grasp the quiet love and piety of her gesture. I felt but could not grasp this gesture, unwavering throughout her lifetime of faith. In that instant, it was simply her nearness—Mom in her Vatican Pavilion Heaven during moments of her witness of exquisite beauty. Rome hardly seemed a worthy spot by comparison.

No Thanks to You

—◦◦◦◦—

You should have figured out the pattern of Dad's anxiety. Why he always said "no" as an initial response, no matter what you wanted to do, where you wanted to go or to ask for clarification? You should have read Mom's silent language, should have noticed your siblings' silence at dinner when you brought something up that you shouldn't have, their eyes downward, their gripping the legs of their chairs or the underside of the kitchen table.

Dad Mantra   You're doing it wrong!
Those words   play without stopping
through sweat   ask myself
What did he say   my brain in knee-jerk phase
in auto-reflex numbness.

You should have realized there was no such thing as good timing. You could have just gone with the flow, ditched trying to do your own thing, and skipped seeking permission rather than forgiveness. You should have learned to be complacent in his presence, to be a convincing liar. You fed his uncertainty, stoked it at every turn.

Age nine   math my nemesis
Dad yells the answer
over and over   his response
over and over   my struggle
over and over   our impasse

Some psychology major you turned out to be. Classic anxiety symptoms, so many Dad's perfect fit. Maybe it was too close to home, to the touch of things. You should have let Mom handle it, watch, and learn her method, her calm, her Libra-balanced calm.

> Body in revolt   red blotches bloom
> spread in wings   down my arms
> across my shoulders
> stomach skin a swarm of measles
> underarms defenseless   skin to skin.

Maybe you kept your psychological competency to yourself because he might have cut off your tuition payments. Or made you switch your major again because he might have thought you were trying to "cure" him.

> I am a breathing hive
> salty tears enflame   my face   in rivulets
> his voice an antigen   my ears pound hard
> Mom's presence ends my night
> No less reddened   no more enlightened.

Those lacking social wires were lines you, Linda, could have tried to detangle. His calm moments were threads of light you could have broadened, his MENSA-worthy intellect a partially mined diamond. You knew his outstanding calm in emergencies was hidden potential. If only you had realized it enough to curry favor with his behavior flaw, perhaps he could have seen his own "emergency" that needed his superb rectifying skills.

> I steal my way to bed
> wishing to die
> between cool linen sheets
> and darkness
> this   the thing I might do correctly.

You know that in the end, his El Dorado shared the same geography as his apprehension. His mathematical prowess was the panacea that granted his selection to the UNIVAC I team in constructing and testing the world's first business computer. Years later, changing the world of Disney World came his way. You know Disney choosing him to design part of the Epcot Welcome Center brushed his fears behind him, trailing as Tinkerbell's wave of motion always does when she darts about the Magic Kingdom Castle.

You know his phobia line resides in you. Your once severe panic attacks have roots, his roots, but you have outpaced that obstacle. Thanks to him, you steer a calmer course.

No thanks to you. You could have been more helpful to Dad.

Spelling Not Required

———⚬❧⚬———

I must admit there are many words and expressions in the Italian language that I never saw in print until I read *The Godfather* at the age of sixteen. It never occurred to me that I would need written proof of Sicilian slang (and curse words). Those phrases just *were*. It took some research to discover how words in my aural memory spell out. My mind clicks into that dormant part of my brain, my limbic ethnic language system. A "sounding it out," from what I remember. My sketchy knowledge of the Italian language called into play.

It is with genuine regret that I never learned the language. My mother's parents, though Sicilian, did not enforce the language within their family. They spoke Italian at home, and their children understood most of what was said, but they would respond to my grandparents in English. As a toddler, I repeated everything I heard my grandparents say, but my parents did not reinforce it at home. Theirs was an attempt, as it was with those around them, to Americanize their children, to have them assimilate into the New World. When one of my uncles met his future wife, he introduced himself with the Americanized version of his name. My aunt never called him by any other name. His tombstone bears it as well, her prerogative.

My grandparents read the Italian newspaper; they were primarily self-taught. Any written English words were sparse to identify packaged items. I still see the word *bread* on a brown paper bag. I still see their signatures on our birthday cards. Nothing more. They learned English from the outside world and their children. Some words, similar in sound in both languages, were a blessing. *Moderazione* (moderation), for example. One of Grandpop Arci's favorite words. *Leenda, everything in moderazione!* he would say.

I know there was no thought on my grandfather's part to abbreviate his surname.

A-R-C-I-D-I-A-C-O-N-O. He was intensely proud of the length of it, one letter short of a dozen. He always reminded us that it meant "Archdeacon." I still smile every time I view its dominance on my grandparents' tombstone.

There might have been some ambivalence within my mother's generation. Italy's switch to the Allied Powers during World War II was more than a crisis in military strategy. It was also one of identity, a wrenching issue from the moment of its inception.

Italians speak two languages: the hands and the words. Our hands disclose our hearts. There are hand movements, words, and phrases that are a part of me for which I make no apologies. We are not a militant group in general, just specific and emphatic. If you doubt how Italians feel about anything, watch our hands. While numerous words and phrases are dear to me, there are four I consider cornerstones.

Yo! As in *hey, or hello.* An attention-getting sound. A South Philadelphian salutation. One of the first words I recall hearing. I thought it was an English word. Perhaps borrowed from the Latin *Io*, an exclamation. The letter "Y" is not part of the Italian language. "Yo" appears in Latin as "Io," with its translation to "Yo" in English. Perhaps Anglicized. The mystery deepens.

Mal Occhio: *Evil Eye*, ingrained in Italians from conception, is a curse extended by a person who casts a jealous eye upon another person. Little old Italian ladies took the Evil Eye seriously; these women concocted remedies to combat it (mustard poultices applied to the chest, for example). Many non-Italians are fully cognizant of this term.

Capisci? Do you understand? Of course, we understood from our crawling stage. This simple word maintains its translation in English via movies and commercials. Of course, with an index finger tap on your temple.

Agita: Aggravation/agitate/acid reflux/heartburn/upset/etc. The greatest word in human language. Multifarious in the degree of meaning intensity. Coupled with hand motion: one hand brought parallel to the mouth, speaker biting the index finger, hissing, eyes flashing, *You give me agita!* No word evokes such fear in a child, with no doubt about what it might mean. *Agita.* A rite of passage word in the hall of language fame. (There is a song bearing the title "Agita," sung by Nick Apollo Forte in the 1984 movie *Broadway Danny Rose.*)

There's also *goomba,* an Americanized anomaly, probably a derivative of *compadre,* a word lesson for another day.

Capisci?

Touchstone Phrases

Italian Proverbs:
> ~Water is good for you, but wine makes men sing.~
> ~When you spit in the air, you get hit in the eye.~
> ~God gives apples to people who have no teeth.~
> ~Never make a toast with an empty wine glass.~

Grandmom Marrone Maxim:
> *~You've got to take the world by the tail.~*

Grandpop Arcidiacono's Philosophies:
> ~The line between happiness and sorrow is small.~
> ~When there's something inside a person, it's in their knuckles, and that will never change.~
> ~A young person can die, but an old person must die.~
> ~Everything in *moderazione* (moderation).~

Grandmom Arcidiacono's Axioms:
> ~If you keep music in your heart, a singing bird will come to you.~
> ~The young woman was beautiful until she opened her mouth.~
> ~What doesn't happen in a hundred years can happen in one day.~
> ~What's wrong is right, and what's right is wrong.~

~Who am I to argue with the truth?~ Uncle Ben Arcidiacono

~It will take you ten years to get over your college education.~ Uncle Vince
   Arcidiacono

Mary Marrone Momism:
   ~Notice how your boyfriend treats his mother.~
   ~Marry a man who likes to dance.~
   ~Always be a good neighbor. Good neighbors are a gift from God.~

Carmen Marrone Conviction:
   ~The truth is the short answer.~
   ~Do not lie to me—ever.~

Aunt Millie Arcidiacono Dinner Mantra:
   ~Kids in the kitchen, adults in the dining room.~

The Children's Response Cheer:
   ~Yesss!!!~

The Italian Pharmacist Platitude:
   ~Good times and bad times come at the same time.~

~I have so little time to shine.~ Carol Di Williams, beloved neighbor.

~Don't forget your roots!~ Cousin Mary Arcidiacono, the family matriarch
   and centenarian.

Nose-talgia

When Grandpop Arci, his friends, and his family came to America from Sicily in the early 1900s, they hid grapevines among their belongings. These grapevines were planted after arriving at a friend's farm in NJ. Some descendants of those scrappy cuttings still survive at the approximate vintage age of one hundred and ten years.

My visits to wine and spirits shops always have a hidden purpose. I search for the color that summons the smell.

Every October, we make wine at my grandparents' house. The date is not set in stone but grapes. Adept neighbors keep their surreptitious distance, expectant of signs of the annual event. The produce truck arrives from the Italian market—grapes in their crates rumble to the little row house on the little street. The rumble signals non-family to their windows; they venture outside to sweep their sidewalks. Crates upon crates of purple goodness, royal purple beads exposed to the Autumn sun. Regal Zinfandel and their mutant cousins, the Moscato green (aka white). The neighbors eye "Tanno," my grandfather, furtively, hoping he shares small clusters of Nature's pearls, counting on his ever-gracious temperament.

The cramped basement needs no preparation; it is already the purple heart of our ritual. We form two congregations. Women are upstairs preparing a regal feast, and men and grandchildren are working below. The primary wine press, ominous yet benign, sits in one corner of the room, the imposing casks on the other. I smell the secret recipe held tight by these sacred vessels. We grandchildren stand stock-still on the stairway, waiting.

Three "Z" red, one "M" white—all a cascade of red, plum, indigo plum, light lime, amethyst, iris, soft purple, chartreuse, rounds pressed into service. Three crates of Zinfandel, one of Moscato per batch.

A long iron lever is the pull to set the process in motion. The Bacchus juice runs out of the press to the gully at the bottom of the barrel. Our male elders scoop the majestic flow, the pace quick to fill the patient grand guardians of fermentation.

To watch Grandpop Arci was a study of hands as peasant and priest, of the mundane and the elegant, preaching temperance.

The hidden purpose of my wine shop visits a search for yet another day. Three red, one white. Color of the smell nowhere in sight.

Three red, one white. Grandpop grips the lever like an oar. He works the press as a limb of his body, his thick, pulsing Renaissance muscles in motion. My father and my uncles are no match for his seamless, athletic movement. The round fruit of the gods deflates to an oozy plum and white pulp, the *Squish! Squish!! SQUISH!!!* a litany, a sigh of relief. Mutant Moscato skins are now unseen yet present and essential.

Grandpop queues his grandchildren to the press. My height and my size place me at the end of the lever. On the count of three, grandpop stands next to me to add his strength and balance. He pulls too quickly; his arm muscles jump like frightened newborn rabbits. I lose my footing, taking my cousins down to the floor with me. The virgin potion hisses through the press, and a stream of purple silk flows past our feet. The lever pitches backward, startled.

∾ᢒᏇᏇᢓ∾

I steer the shopping cart, thinking of the ashtray in my grandparents' house. It read, *Acqua te fa bene, ma vino cantare l'uomone.* Water is good for you, but wine makes men sing. My wine selections fail again to meet the sight-smell test.

∾ᢒᏇᏇᢓ∾

Laughter overhead. The fragrance of our labor intoxicates me. I try to stand up, but the cellar floor keeps moving. The walls pitch and hurl themselves in every direction. I am in a funhouse jumble. I struggle again to my feet. I inhale the color spectrum of violet in its full intensity, deafening, sight-searing. The more I laugh, the more sensory I become. Grandpop guides me to the basement landing. The wooden railing is my life preserver.

Grandpop tells me not to move. He rolls his hazel eyes in a *Grand-mom will kill me if she sees you like this* expression. We both know this Truth. I am an eight-year-old inebriated by inhalation.

The casks are dated and plugged. Grandpop fills his prized decanter from a predated barrel for our evening meal. I remain still. We are the last ones to arrive at the dinner table. My lungs are still in a swell, saturated curtains quietly righting themselves to reoxygenate. Grandpop shares the aged liquid with us. I keep to the far end of the table.

∾ᢒᏇᏇᢓ∾

One day, that color that evokes that smell surprised me during a visit to the Metropolitan Art Museum in New York City. There it was, in the background of a painting of a radiant sunset, a purple-velvet veil, the spellbound smell enrapturing. The staff hurried us out of the exhibit; closing time was near. Artist and title an enigma.

∾ᢒᏇᏇᢓ∾

Inhaling back to this scene, this very dry, dreg-heavy homemade brew has no taste appeal to me. More significant is grandmom's savvy usage of the remaining pulp. Someone referred to these sediments as the *must* of the grapes. She conjures a vinegar dressing from those sediments, the most remarkable mixture to ever grace a salad.

My once immature palate holds the secret flavor forever. I taste it when I see that elusive hue. It seldom occurs, but the synergy is instinctive and involuntary. I remain its private sommelier. My quest continues.

La ricerca ti fa bene, ma trovare ti farà cantare. Searching is good for you but finding will make me sing.

Arrivederci (See You Later)

———⟡———

My siblings and I have no regrets about our time with our grandparents. We hold ourselves in eternal debt to my father, who welcomed grandpop into our home during those last four years of his life. Dad, the son-in-law, loved grandpop with a heart he kept hidden. Grandpop often said he had four sons, not three.

One inclusive memory among us was their goodbye ritual. Whenever we would leave my grandparents' house, they would stand on the top step at their front door, waving goodbye. They stayed there until our car was out of sight. They stood side by side, always in the same position; Grandmom with her full apron to our right, beside her, Grandpop with his cigar soon to be lit. My mother would call them as soon as we arrived home.

My brother and I recently learned that we continue their tradition whenever our children leave our houses. We close our front doors when they are out of our sight. A text arrives when my daughter reaches her destination. The ritual of departure and destination abides.

Ruminations

———◦◦◦◦———

My house on So. 27th Street, the homes of my grandparents, and our church were the cardinal directions of my universe in the 1950s. There were no other places on earth more important.

Back then, small one-way residential streets in South Philadelphia were heartbeats that somehow led to the spacious, two-way business streets. Ours was a row house in the Gray's Ferry area, known unofficially as an "Italian Pocket." While Irish immigrants were more prominent, the neighborhood Catholic churches kept ethnic differences at bay. There were churches for the Italians, the Irish, and the Polish. We self-identified by faith and geography. Everyone lived in parishes and on street corners. You were *from* a parish and *located* at intersections. We were "our pockets." As a child, whenever I heard the pocket phrase, I imagined we were attached to the unseen jackets of our worship places.

The *clink* of pre-dawn milk delivery was the alarm clock of the working class. How could horses and men wake up so early? How thoughtful the dairymen who covered their horses' hooves with fabric to muffle their iron clanking on the quiet predawn street. Many salesmen peddled their trades door-to-door. None was more welcome than the Bond Bread salesman, a pleasant-faced Italian gentleman whose Herculean left arm brandished a colossal basket of heavenly delights. Ah, those confections, handled like jewels, the twinkling icing, the enticing aroma just birthed from the factory nearby!

You could see the entrance to my bedroom from the bottom of the stairway on the first floor. Some might imagine this an obstacle to my sleep. Perhaps it was advantageous. There was no doorbell I couldn't hear at nap time. Mario Lanza's music never prevented nightly rest; his gifted voice wafted from the Hi-Fi player in the living room below. Pleasant tethers of my small world.

⚬◝◯◞⚬

It had to be October 6, 1961, when mom decided to put on her bridal gown to celebrate my parent's tenth wedding anniversary. No book reading for her that night; she glided into my bedroom wearing her wedding dress. The perfect fit, three kids later. Mom made my small bedroom blossom. Her pearled, vaguely beige crown graced her forehead, and her modest veil, yet unravaged by time, trailed past her shoulders to the floor. The bluish hue of her black hair, lustrous as moonlight, in gentle waves, as it was in the photos on that day. No numbered hair dye box could attain such color perfection. The ballet dancers wallpapered around my room, evening bridesmaids surrounding her in diaphanous pastel skirts. I can't recall wishing her a happy anniversary, too overcome at that moment with how beautiful she looked that night. She leaned down to kiss me; a vague trace of Chanel No. 5 entranced my senses. One of my father's last lucid comments many years later was a sigh about her beauty.

I slept with her vision of loveliness under my pillow. From that good night onward, I imagined that eight-year-old me would awaken the following day looking exactly like her. Or perhaps, some morning after.

⚬◝◯◞⚬

My bedroom was different, and so was I. Perhaps our move from South Philadelphia to Roxborough was my first life event shift. Maybe the quick answer was that you're not just ten years old anymore, and you're not in your old neighborhood.

Years after that move, my wonder about some things remained permanent. The teenage me still marveled that two windows framed my spacious bedroom on either side. The adolescent me still marveled that our family lived in this big twin house with a front lawn, a recreation room, four bedrooms, two-and-a-half bathrooms, and a garage. Mine was the room with its own aroma clock, as it was directly above the kitchen. Coffee, eggs, and bacon emissions floated up through my floor every Saturday morning; simmering gravy comforted me during afternoons as I wrote essays and term papers for college. Mom's special occasion cheese pie, long past glorious consumption, still trailing aromatic contentment.

My bedroom became my focal point. I continued my weekly letters to my best friend from South Philadelphia. Our correspondence was most intense and active. This room was my homework headquarters, my vantage point for watching vicious summer lightning storms. The spot where I felt a split-second earth tremor one night during my college sophomore year. The place where my typewriter joined my radio and record player in 1969. This threesome was my solace, the confidants of my private life. The place where my identity evolved, where I felt complete.

~∞Ⓔ∞~

I glanced at the ceiling of the room I knew better than any other room. Three times I counted from one to ten, inhaling and exhaling for calm. I heard dad chewing mom out about the following day, about what time her appointment was. Mom warned me not to worry about this recent nightly ritual. One more minute of this exchange and I would be in their bedroom, diverting dad's escalating tone toward peaceful rest.

Mom needed daily radiation treatments for six weeks during the summer of 2008. A routine examination revealed a small indeterminate growth in her right breast. Her doctor termed it *in situ,* meaning a group of cells in their original place. Potentially cancerous. A daily single radiation beam would zap the growth.

I would ferry her to these appointments. I would spend the evenings with her and dad from Monday through Friday, remaining at their house overnight. The ritual would begin at 5:30 am on those mornings. Chauffeuring mom started the moment my alarm clock sounded. Mom, never one to prepare for an outing with any sense of urgency, needed gentle reminders. Dad's hopping up-and-down temperament and emerging loss of short-term memory required my channeling him to his comfort zone, the living room man's chair. For them, time was insignificant. I paused during those mornings, held the knob of my former bedroom door, and recalled the coffee of my aroma clock days.

◦৹⊙৻৹

There is too much to think about; it is overwhelming. The now-not-ours time is here. Too many dinner celebrations with family and friends to forget in the room that is now-not-ours. Too many memories of grandparents living with us in this now-not-our house.

For all of us neighborhood kids growing up together, there were never too many of us. For all our parents, there were never too few. For all the grass there was, there was never enough to trample. Neighbors who sold their houses told us how it felt when their homes were now-not-theirs. We shut their comments out. *Not ours,* we swore.

◦৹⊙৻৹

We denude the house. We remove the full-sized wall-length mirror from the dining room wall. My growth chart, this mirror, how I measured myself for the first time when I climbed on the couch in our old house and found myself at eye level with its beveled edge. *Mirror, mirror, on the wall, who's the tallest one of all?* Mirror has gone. The room diminishes to a foreign space, truncated, unfocused, and dizzying; this space is now-not-ours.

◦৹⊙৻৹

Mom kisses a farewell to the kitchen and dining room walls, believing no one sees her—as did her father when his home was now-not-his when he came to live with us. As we leave, the new owner arrives, his grateful smile for the beautiful home that is now his. Bedroom doors hinge on new occupants.

As we depart, my sister plays a marching tune from Spotify. I imagine she carved her initials somewhere in the now-not-ours garage, once her makeshift silk-screening studio. I envy the thought.

This Old House

WINTER 2010:
We all grow up, then venture our separate ways: our parents' age, the houses age. Our parents depart for their heavenly place.

My father dies first.

> The "For Sale" sign transplants itself on our lawn.
> The "Sold" sign supplants my American Dream.
> On the final day, mom farewell kisses the walls.
> Farewell kisses to a most beloved child.

Mom thinks I do not see this act.

SPRING 1963:
My mother smiles her way through the door of her mother's house. She announces *We're moving!*

Moving?   Moving!   Moving.

Her words rush over and around me; I am paralyzed. I am ten years old. My heart turns cold. I will never see my best friend again. I tell no one that the "For Sale" sign is a stop sign to the life I knew—a stop sign to what will soon be past tense. My best friend figures it out; my face closes up in fear of losing her. My siblings and I are "farmed out" to relatives who "parent" us until the new house is ready for us to inhabit.

SUMMER 1963:

We move in, one of the first "new families," first owners of the newly constructed American Dream. Released from the cramped former space. Released to grass, wide streets, garages, and driveways. All of us are new kids on the block. I smell that first coat of paint. I smell Saturday morning coffee from the kitchen below my bedroom. I stare at my bedroom ceiling and thank God I am in this place now. I wish my best friend were here with me. Our weekly letters console us.

We kids do not need the new kitchen wall phone; we call out to each other through open windows, the back of our houses facing the driveways. We call it "Outback" now and forever. We yell from wherever we happen to be, *Mom, I'm goin' Outback!*

> Rolling down the hills in boxes, playing dumb like little foxes,
> Broken limbs, scraped knees, daredevils falling out of trees.
> Dirty necks, dirty fingers, radios blaring, bee sting stingers.

We eat water ice (with mustard-plastered pretzels), run through sprinklers, and run on forbidden lawns from early morning till mosquitos bite us home at night.

We watch the new houses appear across the street. Now regretting he gave us too much house for the money, the builder constructs this next group of higher-priced homes smaller in scale. Our American Dream houses are one of a kind.

AUTUMN 1963:

We start school and immediately know we are not welcome. Too many "Eye-talians." Too many of us at one time. Our neighborhood fills the school bus every morning. The school added a new bus with a new route. Unfazed, we do not adjust to the school or the parish. The school and the parish adjust to us. Our weekly church envelopes overspill the parish coffer.

> Steady enders, Double Dutch,
> simple pleasures never cost much.

WINTER 1963:

Mom, I'm goin' Outback!

> We latch our feet to the sled behind us,
> long line zipper   parting the driveway snow.
> Sledding down Devil's Hill, hearts stand still.
> Mr. D. and daughter singing,
> We kids dream what Santa's bringing.

SUMMER 2016:

When mom's hearse passes the house on her final day, I blow a kiss from the car window. I don't want to look, but I do, for the last time. I wonder if mom sees my act. I can no longer pass my American Dream Street.

WINTER 2016:

Over the river and through the woods, avoiding the house, I drive. I'm meeting long-time school friends for lunch. The longest distance to keep me distant is closest to my mind. I circumnavigate my globe, convolution my solution. I add extra travel time to be on time.

Our 'old house' is the new house to the new owner. "Old" dwells in the eye of the homeowner.

Now-Not-Ours

The now-not-ours time has come
far too much to consider
from room to room
cedar closet calls my name.

Dining room summons the aroma
of fantastic feasts with friends and relatives
too many celebrations unforgettable
in the house that is not-now-ours.

Grandpop gives my dad
what he does not have
a twenty-five dollar deposit
for our new home in 1963.

Our American Dream begins here
a childhood strong, a community, a village
Grandpop lives his final years with us
in the house that is now-not-ours.

Our one-of-a-kind neighborhood a haven
never too many of us kids
to grow up together
never too few for parents who raise us.

Years later, neighbors who sell
before us tell us how it feels
when their homes are now-not-theirs.
We shut their comments out, *not ours*, we swore.

Mom RIPs the kitchen and dining room walls
with kisses she thinks no one sees
as grandpop did when he left the home
that was no longer his.

Our path crosses with the new owner
in joy for the beautiful home that is now his.
My sister spotifies a marching tune as we depart
I bet she carved her initials somewhere
in the now-not-ours garage.

No Expectations

———◦⟨⟨⟩⟩◦———

At the end of Grandpop Arci's life, he kept asking me what time it was and what day it was. It is with guilt (still) to confess that this became a little annoying. I overlooked his signal that our time together was approaching its end.

One afternoon, grandpop was in a reflective mood. He told me that if someone had told him when he was young what he would see and experience in his lifetime, he would never have believed what he was hearing. He twirled his right hand in the air. *Pazzi!* (crazy), he chuckled. Man walking on the moon astounded him the most.

After a moment of silence, he continued, *Leenda, I was lucky. Some-day, jobs like mine will be gone. Working with your hands will change to working with your brain. I told your mother from when you were a little girl that you needed an education, that you had to go to college. I am so happy the three of you went.*

◦⟨⟨⟩⟩◦

Later that evening, I checked in on him as he slept. He waved his arms in the air. It was not distracted thrashing; his composure calmed me. As I watched, I dismissed my first thought of his conducting an opera. He was operating the loom he shared his life with, that beloved harp of threads, an aerial mobile as close to his heart as his spouse. His sleep-weaving was graceful, elegant, and caring, unlike the deliberate motion of the lever pull of his winepress. He smiled and finished his work, fingers moved by his side until repose set in.

Expectations

———⟨◈⟩———

When my daughter Eve was a pre-teen, she asked me, *Why didn't your grandparents just go back to Italy? Why couldn't they go just like that, whenever they wanted?*

Just like this, I responded:

1. When your great-grandparents arrived in our country, most private homes did not have telephones.
2. There were no international airplane flights.
3. There was no TV, no Netflix, no Instagram. There were telegrams, usually bearers of bad news for the recipient.
4. Fax machines did not exist. There were no Xerox copiers.
5. No such thing as Facebook. No CD players or YouTube.
6. No indoor plumbing, microwave ovens, air conditioners, or electric blankets.
7. Dishwashers and washing machines were not appliances; they were humans (usually women). The sun and the basement dried the wash. Irons did not operate by electricity; they were metal steamships heating on a stove or filled with boiled water.
8. Automobiles were the exception. Everybody walked everywhere or took trolleys.
9. There were no such things as garbage disposals, computers, instant coffee, disposable diapers, pantyhose, or feminine hygiene products.

10. People would shy away from you if you dared to suggest that
    man would travel to the moon.
11. Penny candy really was a penny.
12. Divorce was rare.

As she pondered my litany, I continued:

*Travel overseas would be by ship, three weeks long one way; the coming
and going and visiting would take two months or more. It was expensive;
there were no credit cards to secure passage. Many jobs were not permanent.
Employers did not extend paid vacations; none would grant this length of
time away from work. If you owned your own business, you needed a trusted
person to continue its operation during your absence. Most people waited
until they retired to visit the homeland. By then, they would visit the children
and grandchildren of many of their beloved deceased family members and
friends.*

After a moment of silence, Eve replied.
Damn!!!

The Forecaster

———⚬⟨◊⟩⚬———

Nothing was more pleasant than making breakfast for Grandpop Arci on Saturday mornings. Mom set her daily routine aside; the kitchen was my domain. Grandpop's simple meal consisted of fruit, a cup of coffee, sometimes accompanied by a biscotti for dunking, and always (over mom's protest) a shot of whiskey. A sly grin would steal its way up the side of his face. Then he would say *I need-a this to get-a my heart moving.*

The meal took a back seat to our quiet conversations. We would chat about family, his garden at the side of the house, and my pending wedding plans. On Saturdays, I diverged from my weekday rushed departure for the bus after kissing him goodbye.

Spring's arrival in 1979 brought a change in subtle ways, most notably in grandpop's mobility. His gait slowed, and his daily rising and bedtime routine were more measured and thorough. He rarely complained. His eyes and hands were his bellwethers.

I didn't give it a second thought when he drummed his fingers on the kitchen table one morning. At his request, I assisted him to his bed, propping him upright. My family relocated his sleeping quarters to the dining room with a cot nearby if he needed us to ease his slumber. Grandpop sighed in comfort, then asked what time it was, recently a habitual question. When I answered him, he looked at me and said, *Leenda, I don't think I'll be hangin' around here much longer.* His calmness warned me not to refute this comment. Old Italian men, who worshipped the words of their Italian wives, also knew of things beyond ordinary comprehension. It was not my place to reproach him. As I sat by his side, he continued, *If I am not-a here next-a year, I promise you it will not-a rain on your wedding day. I will-a take care of it!* He leaned into the pillow and smiled at me.

Grandpop passed away on May 31, 1979. My memory surmises it rained on the day of his funeral, but I remain too bereft to admit, even now, whether it did or not.

～◦⊖◦～

The Sunday before my wedding, the weathermen predicted a hurricane would sweep up from Florida to the Atlantic coast. My father brought the news to my attention. I responded that I was not worried about it, as Grandpop Arci promised me it would not rain on Saturday. As each day passed, the prediction remained unchanged. My father would remind me what was coming, eliciting a smile from me with grandpop's words in my mind. The night before the wedding rehearsal dinner, dad mentioned it again. I reminded him with a grin what grandpop prophesized and added that our church's spacious choir loft would suffice as a dressing area if necessary.

The day did not disappoint. The morning of May 17, 1980, held its beauty from the moment of its dawning. The sky was clear, the wind was absent, and the sun held back its warmth—no mention of hurricanes. The day yielded to a lovely evening, ending far too quickly.

The newlywedded Mr. and Mrs. Kenneth Romanowski stopped at my parent's house to say our final goodbyes for the night. My father walked us to Ken's car. As dad departed, I glanced up at the windshield, noticing a few droplets of *what on earth*—I looked at the dashboard clock. It read 12:01 AM. A light pattern of rain began.

Grandpop!

We beeped the horn at dad. As he turned, I opened the car window, smiled, pointed to the sky, and waved.

The Place of Honor

─────◦⟨⟨◦⟩⟩◦─────

The wreath was on the table. I had just twisted the last piece of florist wire to the frame. My mother admired my handiwork. *Lin, you did a good job; it looks beautiful.*

It was a simple pinecone wreath made of the seasonal foliage I gathered from walks in Fairmount Park with Ken, my fiancée.

The doorbell rang. Ken arrived. We prepared to take a drive to my aunt's house for dinner, driving in two cars. Mom reminded me to be careful with the wreath.

It was December 1979, the first Christmas since my grandfather's death. He died that May. Ken, my siblings, and I decided to stop at the cemetery before celebrating a holiday meal with my aunt and other family members. The cemetery was a short distance from her home.

The short ride to the cemetery seemed longer than usual. I dreaded the thought of stopping there, dreaded the idea of walking among tombstones. I shivered. The shifting of my weight disturbed the wreath. I could feel it moving in the carry bag. I readjusted the bag between my knees, balancing it as the car drove through traffic, navigating turns right and left.

We pulled into the cemetery, driving past each section to our family plot. One of us remarked at the sign at the end of one of the rows. *This road is a dead end.* Seeing this never ceased to unsettle me, each word heavier to read than the one before it.

We walked along the section. None of us wanted to be there. The late afternoon cold settled in and penetrated through the new boots Ken gave me for Christmas. I sighed heavily.

We stopped at our grandparent's tombstone. It was dreadful to look down at those names, the names of two people I had looked up to all my life. My childhood phobia of being underground gripped me. I told myself this was silly; they were dead, not suffocated. I whispered to Ken not to bury me when I die. He recoiled from me and said, *Lin, I know this is hard.* I nodded. I couldn't believe they were both gone. We were silent. It seemed unnatural to be there, to walk among and stand among bodies underground, strangers and loved ones; we, the trespassers of the living. The tombstone held their names:

Sebastiana Arcidiacono

Gaetano Arcidiacono

I smiled to myself. When my grandfather came to America from Sicily, he had no fortune but a surname that he was always intensely proud to pronounce. He let no one Americanize it. With his name came his accent, for, at age eighteen, his native tongue set his speech patterns. It was the same with my grandmother.

Consequently, they never pronounced my name correctly in English; they called me "Leenda." As I looked at their names in the stone, I was glad grandpop hadn't compromised, that the letters and dates left little room on the granite's surface. I was glad they called me Leenda. *Leenda* was one of the first words I recall hearing. Their calling for me still rose from the surface of my memory.

I wish I had known your grandmother, Ken said softly. So did I. Grandmom died in 1974, a year before my college graduation. After a year or so, grandpop came to live with my family. Now, he was gone, a year before my wedding. *She would have loved you*, I answered, struggling for control, *as much as grandpop did.*

Grandmom and Grandpop Arci, as we called them, were unique as a couple and as individuals. Grandmom was petite and stocky, with a lovely face and disposition. Her accent was charming—she even laughed with an accent. She possessed a beautiful singing voice and could ply a sewing and embroidery needle with natural skill. My earliest and most pervasive recollection is her sewing while singing opera, accompanied by the kitchen radio. Moments permanently ingrained into my soul.

The sole purpose of her coming to America was to care for her brother, Antonio. Her family decided that she accompany him. What prompted her parents to send her is lost to history. She also worked in a factory near her South Philadelphia neighborhood, but the location and what she did are unknown. She once told a relative she would not work as a domestic; she did not wish to be anyone else's servant.

Mom asked her once why she spent more time teaching me sewing than she did her. Grandmom would say she was too busy raising her family; I would say the talent skipped a generation. Even with her limited education, grandmom understood enough to laugh at this remark.

Grandmom had her quirky ways too. Her faith and superstition were such that I would tease her that she carried rosaries in one hand and a rabbit's foot in the other. Grandmom completely believed in *Mal Occhio,* the Evil Eye. She believed dreams were the signs and warnings in a person's life, not to be ignored. In her mind, there was no dichotomy between her religion and her cultural heritage. It was an endearing quality.

Then, there was her "cure-all," the Italian elixir to every ailment. Garlic. Garlic for good luck, garlic for colds and fevers, garlic to keep the *Mal Occhio* at a distance. She, and the neighborhood ladies from the old country, were their self-appointed Italian Almanac: predictions, admonitions, and ethnic observances dispersed with their genuine sense of their beliefs.

Grandmom was highly fussy about personal appearance. She made some of her children's clothing from hand-drawn patterns—those outfits were made to perfection. Grandmom never overlooked a detail, especially the shoes. She insisted that everyone's shoes be cleaned and shined at all times. We were sure Grandmom took her fussiness to Heaven with her. We surmised that she upbraided Grandpop as soon as they reunited for not straightening his tie.

Grandpop was grandpop, tall and striking, slow-moving yet deliberate in action. A gentleman. A gentle man. He was a weaver by trade and, with his two brothers, were the most skilled workers at the Frankford

Worsted Mills, a factory located in the east Germantown section of Philadelphia. He could identify all-natural fibers by touch and would tell us whether the clothing we purchased was of good quality. He would describe the weaving process to us, how the patterns were set, the noise, and the dirt involved in creating the finished product. The din of the shuttles left him slightly deaf, yet even with his partial loss of hearing, he insisted that family dinnertime be quiet. He took great pleasure in cooking as well as in eating. In either activity, watching him was a study of hands in the dual role of peasant and priest, of the mundane and the elegant. And always, his hands preached temperance.

Above all, grandpop loved our grandmother. She would pick on him and insist he smoke his cigars in the backyard. He would mumble under his breath in Italian and feign complete deafness. Still, there was no one but Anna for him. In his mind, she was his sweetheart from the first time he saw her. He never forgot to show his love for her during the holidays. He would bring her candy every Valentine's day in a velvet red heart-shaped box, even when they both knew she no longer had much taste for it.

They were married for fifty-six years. Theirs was a devotion Norman Rockwell could have captured on canvas. Their faces would have been a joy for him to paint, these simple people of dignity.

My sister was talking. I heard her say how she loved their house. So did I. Their charming little row house were located on a little street in South Philadelphia. Their backyard spilled over with basil, parsley, and flowers. There was an outhouse in their backyard that intrigued us as youngsters. The prodigious cement planter we grandchildren used as one of the targets for our annual Father's Day watermelon seed spitting contest. The red lantern at the base of the living room stairway that we would play with until grandmom caught us. The ashtray with the Italian worded proverb that read, *Water is good for you, but wine makes men sing.* The Pagliacci doll that endured childhood brawls. The wondrous smells of cooking, baking, and winemaking. Especially the winemaking.

Grandpop made wine every October. It was always a happy time for his neighbors and us. When the grapes would arrive from the Italian market, the rumblings of the produce truck signaled the neighbors to their front doors. Grandpop knew they were waiting for him. Always generous and gracious, he gave away small samples to everyone. The work itself was strictly a family affair. The women congregated upstairs to prepare dinner while the men and grandchildren navigated the process in the basement. On one occasion, the intoxicating fragrance of our labor overcame me. The memory of the basement floor pitching up and down made me chuckle. I reigned in my emotions; the cemetery was no place for laughter. I placed the wreath at the base of the headstone.

~∞∞∞~

My aunt's house was full of relatives. Tables were placed end to end to accommodate everyone, extending from the dining room halfway into the living room. As we ate and drank, our voices rose and fell with good wishes for the holiday, and glasses clinked with emphasis. Most of the credit was my aunt's doing, but I did not praise her efforts immediately. Instead, I teased her. I asked if her traditional family dinner gathering announcement still applied: *Kids in the kitchen, adults in the dining room?*

My aunt answered, *I never thought that sentence would be turned against me!* I teased her, *Well, after all, we are the kids!* We looked at each other and laughed. Her phrase passed through time; it became part of the family verbal archive.

It was a fabulous Italian feast, everything from escarole soup, to lasagna, to Italian rum cake. Ken claimed later that this was the meal that sealed his fate with my family. Love through food. Always love through food.

The conversation among our cousins covered our interpretations of our favorite TV commercials. This raucous activity prompted my uncle to ask why we kids always talked about the same things whenever we were together. There was no answer, except that we always enjoyed discussing the same things.

At one point, there was an uncomfortable silence. One of my cousins asked who threw basil into the grave plot during grandpop's burial service. No one answered; he looked at me. *I know it was you, Lin. That was a great idea. I wanted to laugh. I bet grandpop did. But to this day, I'm sorry no one eulogized him at his funeral Mass.*

⸎

It wasn't that no one thought of it. We were too busy wanting grand-pop to stay alive. To see his strength, the milestone of his life, become a millstone for his demise was a constant struggle for us. To live with someone who became a specter of himself took its toll on my family, to the complete depth of pain as we faced the next move of placing him in a nursing home.

Our last family conference loomed in my mind at that moment. I saw it all again in an instant. My father, the son-in-law, repeatedly said that we could not bear to release grandpop from our loving home. Then, in a matter of days, it was over. Then came these months as our household reknit itself around his absence. The loss ran so profoundly for me; there were moments when I could not hear anything that was said to me at home because I strained to hear grandpop's voice. It was somatic deafness, a behavior that extended to my Saturday morning ventures to the kitchen to make him breakfast, our special time together. My mind would not accept the empty space of that weekend sunshine.

I glanced up from my coffee and smiled at my Uncle John, grandpop's brother. He looked at me with a forlorn yet relieved expression. I knew he was waiting for someone to talk about his brother, whom he adored. I wondered if he realized grandpop was why we had gathered for this meal.

On the way home, we swore the car was heavier because of our abun-dant consumption. This meal will always remain in my memory as the Italian feast of overcompensation.

⸎

We parked our cars and removed the packages of holiday leftovers. We dragged the last bag into the house. Ken sat at our kitchen table to catch his breath before driving home. I picked up the bag that held the wreath. I heard a noise.

What on earth? I reached into the bag and pulled out a pinecone. Then I remembered something I hadn't thought of in a long time. I giggled, then I laughed. My laughter increased; I couldn't stop myself. My family couldn't figure out what was so funny. My face turned red; tears rolled down my cheeks. Ken became alarmed. He thought the day overwhelmed me. I pulled myself together and explained that when we were little, grandpop would tease us during dessert. As we sat together at the table, he would call our name and put a grape or a piece of candy at our elbow before we could catch him. When I found the pinecone in the bag, the memory rushed up inside me. *He had done it again.* I remembered that the time came when we had turned the tables on him and how he laughed with glee that we could trick him too. Now, it seemed we had completed the circle.

I resumed my laughter, such a soothing recollection. Some of my family were skeptical, but I saw it as a sign. Ken observed my behavior as the best it had been in months. I didn't care what anyone thought. *I believed.* And deep down, I think my family did too.

Before I went to sleep that night, my thoughts drifted over the day. It was a blessing to be an older grandchild as my memory of my mother's parents is more complete than my younger cousins. I knew my grandparents as real people; I matured into adulthood, and they were there for me. So many people told me I was lucky. It was true. The traditional commercial view of grandparents only in the company of young children was a myth in our family. Their great-grandchildren were the little ones.

That was a meaningful Christmas, that first holiday season when there was no aroma of cigar smoke in our house. It was important because I felt the true gift of my grandparent's love through my grief. They loved us all, and they still did. Each of us was important and special to them. Their lasting gift to us was the gift of their time, our gift to them, honoring their memory. They were the respite when parents became challenging to raise. In their wise, formally uneducated way, they knew more than we ever will. They had the advantage that most of their lives were behind them when we were born. They guided us without the hurried preoccupation that parents sometimes show because they were busy being parents. Our grandparents experienced a long life together, yet theirs were the eyes and the hearts of children. I never loved them more than during that Christmas.

I made a promise to myself the following Christmas, my first as Ken's spouse. Ken and I kept the promise. We laced a red ribbon on the errant pinecone and hung it on our Christmas tree next to the tree-top angel. (Red was grandpop's favorite color.)

Grandpop, it's Leenda! I whispered.

And every year since then, the pinecone rests beside the tree-top angel at the top of our Christmas tree.

Upbraiding

I had always envied my grandmother's braids. They were silver-gray tresses of beauty, wound modestly around the crown of her head. Ethnic protocol dictated that Italian ladies never allowed their hair to be undone in public once they were married. Wives reserved their flowing hair for private times with their spouses.

But there was one moment, toward the remaining years of my grandmother's life, during my early college years, when she loosened her hair in my presence. She slowly weaved a hairpin through her silvery grey strands, musing, almost as if I weren't there. She spoke, almost under her breath, mainly in Italian, the repetitive phrase that her hair *had gotten her into trouble*. Grandmom sighed, *Oh, Leenda!*

Three months before commencement, my college holds a "One Hundred Days til Graduation" party. THE party of parties, a knock-down, dragged-out hen party held in the cafeteria. In 1975, my college was an all-female institution. Some of us danced unsteadily on the tables. Some of us dance unsteadily on the not-wide-enough windowsills. The music followed its predictable hit parade, then slowly, seamlessly, in undisputed cue, slid backward in time to every dance ever learned, from the Bunny Hop to the St. Vitus Dance.

My best recollection of this family story over a century ago came in sparse fragments from my mother. It was about her mother's education. There was not much grandmom was willing to share, as she was a very private person. Mom knew questioning anything her mother told her about this subject would forever close the issue. In sporadic bits, what mom could tell me was said with a tone that mirrored her mother's tone toward her. I was to listen and not to ask. Not ever. Bits of phrases would come my way now and then until grandmom set her hair free in my company that day. Grandmom, little Anna, that day, in halting, jumbled Italian, mumbled the one part I had never heard before.

Early mornings were the coolest part of the day, the house at its quietest. The windows ushered in the most welcomed breezes. Still, it was mighty hot under that table, and the tablecloth placed over it en-shrouded little Anna and made her claustrophobic surroundings more oppressive as the days came and went. On that first day, her attention was not distracted by the semi-dark, secret atmosphere. She calmed herself in quiet concentration, riveted to what she could only hear but could not see. She heard the door open and bang shut, a room away from where she was hiding. Footsteps came toward the doorway and paused there. She strained toward the voice of a man, the tutor, who spoke authoritatively and relentlessly from his post. Footsteps rushed to their seats at the table at his command.

That summer day, when I was four years old and an unruly handful, my father took me off my mother's hands. We took a walk, dad hoping he would wear out my temper and be ready to nap when we returned home. He thought the two-block walk to our church and back should do it.

As we approached the front of the building, we saw something flut-tering on the top step. As we drew closer, we noticed it was a book, the pages rustled back and forth with the warm breeze. I pulled my hand from dad's sweaty palm, bounded towards it, grabbed one end, and gave it to him. There were children and a dog on its cover. Dad said, *Good, it's a Dick and Jane book.* Naptime was the last thing on my mind when we arrived home. It was time for my first reading lesson.

✿

The tutor began the day's lesson. Now his voice was above her: her siblings, perhaps other relatives or neighbors, reciting and spelling words. From below, little Anna used her right index finger to trace markings on the white damask linen, her blackboard, before her. There were a few words she knew how to spell from one-word signs posted in her town. She had enough self-reliance to know that she would not forget her tracings, was wary enough to sense when the hour's lesson would come to an end, cautious enough to know when she could take her leave unobserved. These clandestine classes went on for many days, probably weeks. The reveal of her hiding place, that matter-of-time-moment, unknown to her.

✿

There is a great deal of laughter and singing during the Hundred Days Party. The louder the music, the more boisterous it becomes. Our classmates include those in their Junior year, a rite of passage. Our college is small, around five hundred in number, and everyone knows everyone, at least by sight. Many Juniors were close friends with the Seniors; some were related. One of the highlights is our class tagline, sung in relentless chorus:

> *The only girls who are alive are in the Class of '75,*
> *The only girls who are alive . . . are in the Class of '75.*

There were haves and have-nots. I was a commuter, a "day hop," a have not. The residents didn't know much about me, but they knew one thing. I sat in the front of every class. Another student, a friend one year ahead of me, did too. And so we had a reputation.

Someone in the room, whose presence never made me comfortable, asks if I will bequeath my front seat in all my classes to a "Sister Junior."

This person is a bit intoxicated. My tipsiness forgives her veiled remark of contempt. My tipsiness does not cloud my presence of mind; I realize even to the end of our time here that no one's behavior escapes notice in a small school. I reign in my tongue. I laugh in reply; I keep chanting our tagline.

⁓◦⊙◦⁓

Mom read me a bedtime story every night. By the time I was five, I knew most of them by heart. I followed her right index finger with my own. In time, the curvy squiggles and big strokes of angled lines took shape, made sense, more minor a mystery, still a mystery. A mystery that I pleased my parents with what I could do. I identified all the little characters on the back of the Golden Books. I'd name each one out loud at the end of each story.

One night, mom was exhausted. She had three children by then. As she approached the bottom page of a fairy tale, she decided to skip some sentences. As she turned the page in haste, I exclaimed, *Mommy, you made a '-stake!* After a muffled laugh, she replied, *Sorry! My mistake!*

⁓◦⊙◦⁓

My fourth-grade classroom was packed with seventy-six students and one door. Our seating arrangement was in strict height order. As one of the tallest children, my seat was dead last in the fifth row, in the center of the room. The vinyl accordion coat closet doors met squarely at the back of my chair. Rainy days were worse than cold weather. The damp coats, soggy boots, and dripping umbrellas created a condensed wet scent as the doors expanded and contracted as the days came and went.

Every afternoon, the class read from textbooks on various subjects. One by one, we stood up, book in hand, to read one paragraph. Reading aloud was my favorite part of the day. When a few new students became classmates, the seating arrangements changed. My place didn't, but the teacher switched the person in front of me to the next aisle. It was immediately obvious that this little girl read at a snail's pace. Since we were in the middle of the classroom, it didn't matter which side of the room read first. The day was over when the clock above the blackboard struck 3:00 P.M.

Every day I eyed the clock, hoping for the chance to read aloud. Every day the same result; the little girl read the last word of the paragraph the moment the clock struck the third hour. One afternoon, several students were absent. *Now's my chance!* I thought. I could barely breathe. The students in my aisle read their paragraphs one by one. My heart beat with joy with each passing word. Ten minutes to go. The little girl in front of me stood up. My heart thuds to the floor. The little girl forgot her glasses. She read at a glacier pace.

The bell rang. Strike three for me.

The unflinching heat weighs the white tablecloth like a suffocating shroud, more a nemesis than usual this day. Little Anna scoots as far as she can to the side of the table that catches the occasional breeze and curls its way up the fabric, providing relief. This breeze allays the smell of the tight warmth and the cloy of the humidity. She removes enough clothing to remain modest. She loosens the braids of her hair to release the sweat. She bares her feet and draws her legs close to her petite frame. The footsteps of the tutor and children approach the room. She poises her seven-year-old arms for the day's lesson.

The thick envelope arrived. In those days, a thick envelope was good news. My acceptance letter and required paperwork came from the college of my choice, Rosemont College, in Bryn Mawr, Pennsylvania. The stunning relief is still a vivid memory.

It happened that one of my relatives stopped by our house that weekend. My parents shared our good news. While they chatted, I entered the kitchen unnoticed. This relative had just commented that sending a girl to college was a waste of time. It was a waste of my time and their money; in the end, I'd *end up pregnant and behind the kitchen sink.* By then, everyone had noticed my presence. I side-glanced at my father. I took advantage of his too-stunned-to-respond look. My calm demeanor revealed no fire to my fury. *This is what I need to do,* I replied.

Before I could continue, my relative interjected, *Okay, let's say you had a twin brother, and your parents had enough money to pay one tuition. What do you think would happen?* Well aware that a female relative gave up her dream and went to work to support her brother's education, I respectfully countered, *Then both of us would split the money, pack a lunch bag under our arms and work to pay the difference.*

Affronted, this person affirmed, *That would never happen in my house.* My mind snapped its mental fortitude with my response, *Then it's really a good thing I'm not one of your daughters!* My father's brandished hand slap was too far away to hit my cheek, but I felt this second blow as if he had struck me. I left the room seething. Two thoughts hit me simultaneously: my father's waving an invisible diploma in the air, lamenting that he never got *that piece of paper.* And that of Grandmom Arcidiacono's legacy burned into my heart.

∽◦◉◦∾

Little Anna knew this day was the day of numbers. It sounded like the man was discussing addition. She knew about drawing sum lines and computation marks from previously written exercises carelessly left behind on the floor. Papers rustled over the children's bored murmur of their lessons. She leaned back to steal some air from a fold of her linen sanctuary, unaware that one of her braids peaked out from the end of the tablecloth that she had tied to the far end of the table leg.

That's when she felt a seismic yank that started from the nape of her neck. Anna was half swung up into the air; strands of her hair loosened with the impact.

The tutor bellowed: *Chi è questo?!?!* (Who is this?)

Too shaken to move, little Anna, quaking in fear, said nothing. Her parents appeared, and the tutor let her loose. Her luxuriant, errant, chestnut brown braids unraveled in a silent confession, the guilty culprits of her crime.

The tutor shrieked at her father. *Your child has been under this table, listening to me teach the others! I must be paid for her as well!* Anna's father, my maternal great-grandfather, remonstrated that he was unaware of her hiding place.

Little Anna, in her mother's arms, teary eyes cast downward, caressed her braids in her hands as if they were wounded birds, her informal education thwarted for life.

On that beautiful May 1975 day, when I stepped up to the stage to receive my college diploma *cum laude,* I extended my hand for my piece of paper. As a first-generation female recipient, I do so not just for me, not just for my parents, not just for my family, but primarily for little Anna. My Grandmother, little Anna, Sebastiana Messina Arcidiacono, who never had the opportunity to sit at the front desk of any class, who encapsulated herself under a tableclothed table to eavesdrop on what education she could.

Perhaps my classmate's remark at the Hundred Days Party enlightened me to my penchant for classroom seating preference. Sitting in the front of the room wasn't really about avoiding the back-of-the-room smokers. I bear her neither grudge nor malice. Her insult may have been conscious, but it might also have come from inebriation, her flirtation with intoxication. If nothing else, it resurrected a memory of little Anna that drove my commencement to a far more profound level. I am grateful for this.

On another beautiful May day in 2015, my daughter Eve graduated from Rosemont College. Before her celebratory "walk" with her classmates, I parked my car at the cemetery and walked to my grandparents' grave. A smiling angel sits on the top of their tombstone. I placed a small, tasseled graduation cap over the angel's shoulders. The wings steady the cap on the statue's head. I know my grandparents know my child shares my alma mater. I know they know she outshines me and that she will graduate *magna cum laude in honoris causa.*

As I write these words, as a Rosemont College MFA candidate, as I reach for my diploma on another May day in 2021, I will hear my grandmother say ever so wistfully, *Oh, Leenda! My hair, my hair, got me into so much trouble.*

Repurpose

POEM DIVIDER

PART I
Among the weeds behind the shed
I protected you from overgrowth, wine press
I saw to that—covered your remains
when someone casts our family history aside

perhaps not thinking or thought
of too much pain
I shielded you, small still
you, once so vibrant

your sturdy, rusted bands
few   hold eager curve
gully lip in proud spout pose
firm   ready to bear juice weight, not rot

the song of squish *squish!*
waits around your rim
splits of oak ache for uva scent
all that you were   you still are.

PART II

So far down
beneath this wood
You, tiny stalk
I find from nowhere

where were you all this time
burrowed beneath   into   around
my remains of memory
in splintered timber

you sowed yourself into
this secret bower
once grape full
of ferment in the dark

you, tendril curl,
before you found this remnant
were you waiting for its move
from corroded darkness into light

were you hoping I might find you
leave you   in your hiding spot
tender your slow growth around the spindle
bring you both back to life with my tears

and wait to see who you are
endive   parsley   arugula

Sudden Matriarchy

My father's second sister
dies this year
why should I be
surprised
her life would end

My memory hears another aunt say
at every family meal
~Kids in the kitchen,
Adults in the dining room~
We cheer   no banishment for us!

I   never in a hurry
to grow up
now   not in a hurry
to grow old
Maturity.   Is.   Here.

Time to be
in the front row
no rows in front of me—
reluctant Matriarch
Resisting.   The.   Horizon.

Acknowledgments

———◦◦◦———

When long-time friend, Scott Leff, tells you your family recollections should be shared, you acknowledge his advice. When Carla Spataro, Rosemont's MFA Director and Advisor, has never led you astray, you stay the course.

I could not have proceeded without my beloved family, my husband Ken, and my daughter Eve, for their unflinching encouragement and devotion. To my siblings, Roseanne and Ralph Marrone, and other family members, I remain thankful for their support. Likewise, I extend grateful acknowledgment to my friends who have given me a wide berth of understanding for my silence these recent months yet supported me completely, nonetheless. I remain forever grateful for the reconnection with my friend Carole Jesiolowski, whose perspective and sense of humor remained peerless and steadfast through the ups and downs of the creative process.

I wish to acknowledge Professor Kristina Moriconi, whose timely arrival in my life at a Rosemont College studio course changed me forever. Your thoroughness as an instructor and mentor instilled in me not to neglect the sense of smell, the use of white space, and the relief of "perhapsing." Your introduction to Mary Karr's work has time-stamped my thought patterns. Your suggestion to refer to Dudley Randall's layout of his book, *Roses and Revolutions,* was a guiding force in assembling this thesis.

I am blessed that my paths have crossed with Teresa Fitzpatrick, J.C. Todd, Tawni Waters, Jillian Sullivan, Jennifer Steil, Erin Entrada Kelly, Margo Rabb, Ayesha Hamid, Grant Clauser, Liz Abrams-Morley, T. Nicole Cirone, Artress Bethany White, Kirwyn Sutherland, Chad Frame, Susi Kimbell, Jennifer Rieger, Jordan Blum, Rae Pagliarulo, Larry Robin, Kris McCormick, and Pat Ciarrocchi. It would be rude to overlook the Rosemont College Library staff, especially Kathleen Deeming and Elena Sisti, whose interest in my endeavor kept my passion for following my dream. A special mention to Julianna Baggott, whose critique of one of my essays revealed the essential quandary, *Whose story is this?* That was a pivotal moment of restructuring and revising, finally conquered.

To my Rosemont MFA classmates, Warrior Writers, who maintain the courage of their convictions: Watsuki Harrington, Meg Ryan, Ann O'Neill, Kyle Robertson, Tyler Kline, Cory Thornton, Christopher Eckman, Rachel Kolman, Sharon Reid, Matt Conte, Dan Crawford, Keith Fallows, Megan Yates, Liz Cunningham, Laura Jackson, Nicolette Pizzigoni, Carlos Perez Samano, Kourtney Gush, Sawyer Lovett, Sara Karasek, Alea Giordano, Celeste Cosme, Christopher Nosal, Nicolette Pizzigoni, Angelina Corleone, Sarah Levine, and Beth Moulton, may she rest in peace. Without your presence, my own would be lacking. Of exceptional note is Jacqueline Jewell, my early "press agent," who was instrumental in guiding me in self-confidence and self-promotion.

To Christine Salvatore, my thesis advisor and poetry professor, whose calm and joyful encouragement was an ever-present inspiration, and for those zoom moments when certain passages weren't "landing right."

I extend my heartfelt thanks and gratitude to the staff of Sunbury Press. My initial meeting with Lawrence Knorr at the 2019 Push to Publish conference began a series of events that has brought me to this moment. Taylor Berger-Knorr has been the consummate navigator and professional whose talent in transitioning writers from one contact to another is peerless. Joe Walters, Marketing Administrator, remained a guiding influence in his genuine interest in my success. Frankie Reed could not have been more excited than I was in preparing the book cover of *Final Touchstones*. Crystal Devine, your book design skill is paramount to the reader's first impression for which there is no second chance. Thank you for your cheerful tenacity, particularly with the challenge of presenting family vintage photographs.

And above all, a special thank you to Abigail Henson, my editor, who has worked with me in the spirit of camaraderie. You never made me feel threatened by your expertise and sound advice. You never caused me angst that my intent would be lost. Finally, to my deceased family members, kept alive weekly via Covid-era telephone conversations with my now deceased centenarian cousin, Mary Arcidiacono Bonanno. May you, my heart touchstones, rest in the peace of my words and your accomplishments.

Publications

"Pot It's Not" was published by *City Key Zine* on 11/25/2018.

"SGPS Global Studies Journal" was published on the Rosemont College website, www.Rosemont.edu on August 22, 2019, and on the RoCo online magazine.

"Empty Venue Full House" was published by *City Key Zine* on 12/02/2020

"The Election That Changed the World" was published by *City Key Zine* on 2/15/2021

"Empty Venue Full House" was published by *City Key Wordpress* on 12/02/2020.

"Christian Street Caruso" was published by *City Key Wordpress* on 1/31/2021.

"Christian Street Caruso" was published on the *Mario Lanza Institute* Facebook page on 01/31/2021.

"Charge of the Night Brigade" was published on the *City Key* Facebook page on 2/13/2021.

"Year of the Ox" was published on the *City Key* Facebook page on 2/13/2021.

"Seen in Translation" *Protest 2021 100 Thousand Poets for Change* was compiled by Moonstone Press on September 2021.

"Pulp Slicktion" was published by *Ovunque Siamo* on 11/1/2021.

"What is in the Blood" was published by *Philadelphia Stories* on 10/03/2021.

"Give or Take Story No.447: It's Been a Hard Day's Recollection" was published by Vine Leaves Press, on 1/27/2022.

"The Eagle and Mrs. B" was published by *City Key Zine* on 12/6/2021.

"Sons of Sicily" and "Field Exile" was published by *Ovunque Siamo* on 2/01/2022.

"The Year of the Tiger" was reposted by the *City Key* Facebook page on 2/01/2022.

"New Beginnings" *International Women's Day Poetry Anthology* was compiled by Moonstone Press on 2/27/2022.

"Ukraine Unwarred" *Ukraine Poetry Anthology* was compiled by Moonstone Press on 3/2022.

"To Kamila Valieva" *Welcome to Philadelphia Poetry Anthology* was compiled by Moonstone Press on 3/2022.

"Nebulae Nocturne," "Moroccan Silent Art," "Night in Marrakesh Medina," "Ocean Caravan at Essaouira," and "Next Generation Pending" *International Haiku Day* were compiled by Moonstone Press on 4/10/2022.

"In Defense of Earth" *Earth Day Anthology* was compiled by Moonstone Press on 4/2022.

"What Hands and Minds Have Wrought" *International Workers Day Poetry Anthology* was compiled by Moonstone Press on 4/2022.

"Some Mushrooms are Ominous" *Hiroshima Day* was compiled by Moonstone Press on 8/2022.

"Enough" *Banned Book Week* was compiled by Moonstone Press on 9/2022.

"It's Been a Hard Day's Recollection" *The 50-Word Stories of 2022* was published by Vine Leaves Press on 10/2022.

"Defying Extinction" was published by *Ovunque Siamo* on November 1, 2022.

"Sears Had Everything" and "Santa Matt" were published by *City Key Zine* on December 17, 2022.

About the Author

LINDA M. ROMANOWSKI is a 2021 Rosemont College MFA Graduate in Creative Writing (Non-Fiction). She received the President's Medal. Her debut heritage memoir and thesis, *Final Touchstones*, is available from Sunbury Press. She is a contributing feature writer for *The City Key*, a former assistant editor for *Rathalla*, and a submission reader for *Philadelphia Stories*, the Sandy Crimmins National Prize for Poetry, and the McGlinn Fiction Prize Contest. Living in Ardmore, Pennsylvania, she concluded her role as president of the Rosemont College Alumni Board in June of 2022.